YASUZO NOJIMA
AND CONTEMPORARIES

The exhibition is curated by Shinji Kohmoto, curator of The National Museum of Modern Art, Kyoto with Jeffrey Gilbert, independent curator and former research assistant of The National Museum of Modern Art, Kyoto, and co-curated by Yuri Mitsuda, assistant curator of The Shoto Museum of Art.

表紙： 野島康三氏 (部分) 1930
錦古里孝治作
ブロムオイル・プリント

COVER： Mr. Yasuzo Nojima (detail) 1930
by Koji Nishigori
Bromoil Print

野島康三とその周辺
日本近代写真と絵画の一断面

京都国立近代美術館

YASUZO NOJIMA AND CONTEMPORARIES
One Aspect of Modern Japanese Photography and Paintings

The National Museum of Modern Art, Kyoto

野島康三とその周辺

京都国立近代美術館
1991年9月10日（火）——10月13日（日）
主催——京都国立近代美術館
協力——野島康三遺作保存会／財団法人堂本印象記念近代美術振興財団
／財団法人花王芸術文化財団／ハイネケン・ビール

YASUZO NOJIMA AND CONTEMPORARIES

The National Museum of Modern Art, Kyoto
September 10—October 13, 1991
organized by The National Museum of Modern Art, Kyoto
in cooperation with The Nojima Collection/Insho Domoto Memorial
Foundation for Modern Art/The Kao Foundation for The Arts/
Heineken Beer

野島康三とその周辺

東京展
渋谷区立松濤美術館
1991年7月16日(火)——9月1日(日)
主催——渋谷区立松濤美術館
協力——野島康三遺作保存会

京都展
京都国立近代美術館
1991年9月10日(火)——10月13日(日)
主催——京都国立近代美術館
協力——野島康三遺作保存会／財団法人堂本印象記念近代美術振興財団
／財団法人花王芸術文化財団／ハイネケン・ビール

YASUZO NOJIMA AND CONTEMPORARIES

Tokyo
The Shoto Museum of Art
July 16—September 1, 1991
organized by The Shoto Museum of Art
in cooperation with The Nojima Collection

Kyoto
The National Museum of Modern Art, Kyoto
September 10—October 13, 1991
organized by The National Museum of Modern Art, Kyoto
in cooperation with The Nojima Collection/Insho Domoto Memorial
Foundation for Modern Art/The Kao Foundation for The Arts/
Heineken Beer

謝辞

この展覧会の調査と準備に当たり、下記の方々からの資料提供、情報紹介のご協力を得ました。ここに記し、深く感謝いたします。

青木　茂
浅野　徹
飯沢耕太郎
伊砂利彦
金子隆一
岸田鶴之助
北村善平
窪島誠一郎
ツアイト・フォトサロン
東京都美術館資料室
藤井利雄
吉川富三
時の美術社
日動画廊
ジェフリー・ギルバート

所蔵者一覧

ひろしま美術館
ブリヂストン美術館
メナード美術館
下関市立美術館
雅陶堂ギャラリー
宮城県美術館
群馬県立近代美術館
財団法人清春白樺美術館
財団法人中野美術館
新潟県美術博物館
真鶴町立中川一政美術館
神奈川県立近代美術館
大原美術館
東京国立近代美術館
野島康三遺作保存会／京都国立近代美術館寄託
ギャラリー新居
萬鐵五郎記念館
日本大学芸術学部写真学科

Acknowledgements

As with any exhibition of this scale and scope, many people have been extraordinarily helpful in providing information and facilitating introductions. We would like to thank, collectlvely and individually, the following :

Shigeru Aoki
Tohru Asano
Kohtaro Iizawa
Toshihiko Isa
Ryuichi Kaneko
Tsurunosuke Kishida
Zenpei Kitamura
Seiichiro Kuboshima
Zeit Foto Salon, Tokyo
Art Library of Tokyo Metropolitan Art Museum
Toshio Fujii
Tomizo Yoshikawa
Tokino Bijutsusha
Nichido Gallery
Jeffrey Gilbert

Lenders of works

Hiroshima Museum of Art
Bridgestone Museum of Art
Menard Art Museum
Shimonoseki City Museum
Gatodo Gallery, Tokyo
Miyagi Museum of Art
Gunma Prefectural Museum of Modern Art
Kiyoharu Shirakaba Museum
Nakano Art Museum
Nigata Prefectural Museum
Nigata Prefectural Museum of Art
Kazumasa Nakagawa Art Museum, Manazuru
The Museum of Modern Art, Kamakura
Ohara Museum of Art
The National Museum of Modern Art, Tokyo
Photographs from The Nojima Collection courtesy of The National Museum of Modern Art, Kyoto
Gallery Nii, Osaka
Yorozu Tetsugoro Museum
Nihon University, Department of Photography, College of Art
Saegusa Gallery, Tokyo

目次

Table of Contents

あいさつ

野島康三（1889-1964）は、大正期の絵画主義写真全盛の時代
と、昭和初期から始まる新興写真の時代の双方にわたって活躍し
た、わが国近代写真の誕生と展開において最も重要な作家のひとり
です。

初期の野島は、ピグメント印画において卓抜した技術と繊細な感覚
を発揮し、非常に密度のある作品を作り上げました。彼の肖像、裸
婦、静物の作品は、対象の存在を極めて深部でつかみ、伝統でも
も外来でもない独自の美学を獲得しました。深い精神性をたたえた
それらの作品は、当時の写真家や画家たちに大きな影響を与えまし
たが、近年再びその評価が高まっています。

絵画主義写真は「芸術写真」と呼ばれ、絵画の模倣に過ぎないと
批判されたこともありましたが、野島の作品は単なる絵画の様式的
模倣に終わらない、写真独自の芸術性を主張するものでした。また
野島は、同時代の美術の熱心な擁護者でもあり、本質的にそれら
を理解したすぐれた視る人でもあったのです。彼は1919年に兜屋
畫堂を開設、梅原龍三郎、中川一政ら当時の新進気鋭の美術家
たちの個展を開き、自宅のサロンでも岸田劉生、萬鉄五郎らの重
要な展観を催しています。野島は彼らと親しく交際し、その芸術に深
く共鳴し、共に同時代の精神を分かちあいながら自己の作品制作
を行いました。本展は、特に関係の深かった梅原龍三郎、岸田劉
生、中川一政、萬鉄五郎の絵画作品をあわせて展示し、野島へ
の影響関係のみならず、時代に胎動する共通の意識を見るととも
に、絵画と写真との関係をも再考しようとするものです。

1932年に雑誌『光画』を発刊した野島は、ドイツ新興写真に傾倒
してゆきます。後期の野島は、重厚なピグメント印画から作風を大
きく変え、瞬間的な感覚をとらえた、シャープで実験的なゼラチンシ
ルバー・プリントの作品へと進みます。そこには、急激な近代化の
なかで、劇的に変貌する作者の感覚が読み取れるでしょう。その頂
点ともいえる個展、1933年の「写真・女の顔20点」は、高い評価
と大きな話題を呼びました。

本展では、野島康三の活動を、初期・後期に分けた代表作104点
で紹介し、上記の4人の画家たちの絵画約36点とともに展覧して、
野島芸術を立体的に回顧いたします。

本展開催にあたりまして、多くの方々のご協力をいただきました。野
島康三遺作保存会をはじめ貴重な作品をご出品下さいました所蔵
者各位、ご協力いただきました関係者の皆様、野島康三の作品研
究と再評価のために長年にわたり御尽力されてきた写真研究家ジ
ェフリー・ギルバート氏に、心から感謝の意を表します

1991年

渋谷区立松濤美術館
京都国立近代美術館

Foreword

Yasuzo Nojima's (1889-1964) activity in the pictorial photography of the Taisho era and the modern photography movement in the first 20 years of the Showa period is just cause for him to be considered among the foremost artists to have worked with photography in Japan.

His early use of pigment printing techniques reveals a great fluency and delicate sensibility, the work truly possesses a refined quality of presence. In his portraits, nudes, and still lifes he sought to discover the essential nature of the subjects existence, exhibiting a personal aesthetic that is neither conventional nor borrowed. Nojima's works are informed by a life-long pursuit of self knowledge, and evidence a broad range of cultural and aesthetic influences shared in common with the other artists of his time. Given the purpose to correct our historical memory, his works are currently enjoying a widespread reappraisal. Pictorial photography has often been stereotyped and refuted as a simple mimicry of painting. Nojima's work, however, does not merely appropriate painterly mannerisms, but stands instead as a positive assertion of the struggle of an artist to define themself. As an advocate for the arts, Nojima developed a keen understanding of his contemporaries' works. In 1919, he opened a gallery named Kabutoya Gado, and mounted one-person exhibitions of up-and-coming artists like Ryuzaburo Umehara and Kazumasa Nakagawa. Later at the salon he founded at his residence he held noteworthy exhibitions for other artists including Ryusei Kishida and Tetsugoro Yorozu. Many of the experiences they shared are central to the formative years of the establishment of modern art in Japan. In order to enable our access to their affinities and pursue the nature of their endeavors, this exhibition includes period examples of paintings by Kishida, Nakagawa, Umehara and Yorozu.

In 1932 Nojima launched the magazine *Koga* (Light Pictures), in which he demonstrated his interest in the international developments of the new photography movement. At one moment he stepped outside the confines of the highly intentional discipline of his pigment printing technique and recontextualized his approach through the modern media of the gelatin silver print. The sudden denial of handwork and applied surface served to align one aspect of his work with the media formalism that pervades and defines fundamental characteristics of the new photography. By extension these characteristics are often said to symbolize the transitory nature of the modern age. In 1933 Nojima's exhibition *Photographs of Womens Faces* saw a peak of this expressive content on a new conceptual basis, and garnered high praise and popular acclaim.

In presenting a comprehensive retrospective of Nojima's art, this exhibition will chart the course of his career, introducing 104 of his photographs together with 40 works of the above four painters.

In conjunction with this exhibition we have received the cooperation of numerous individuals. We offer our heartfelt appreciation to The Nojima Collection, to all of the lenders who have kindly shared their precious works, to the many participants who have lent their assistance, and to Jeffrey Gilbert whose many years of research in the history of photography have served to encourage a reevaluation of the work of Yasuzo Nojima.

The Shoto Museum of Art, Shibuya
The National Museum of Modern Art, Kyoto

左から岸田劉生、野島康三、河野通勢／1922

野島康三序論

ジェフリー・ギルバート

この小論は野島康三についての概論として書き始めるが、その前に、私の個人的な話を少し記す事をお許しいただきたい。

私が続けてきた野島康三に関する調査研究は、学術的とは言い難いものであり、当然ながら私自身の能力も、本稿で紹介する人々の才能には遠く及ばない。私のつたない力では、多項目にわたって収集してきた膨大な資料の山から、ほんの微かな声しか聞き取ることができなかった。1976年に私は、日本における美術と写真との関係とその展開について興味を覚え、独自の調査を始めた。翌年、私はハナヤ勘兵衛氏と出会い、彼から野島康三の写真作品を初めて紹介されたのであった。ハナヤ氏は今世紀初頭に生まれ、1930年代前半にその才能を開花させた写真家であり、創造力において当時の写真家たちの頂点に在った野島康三の作品と活動から、計り知れない啓発を得た人物である。ハナヤ氏はあらゆる機会をとらえ、野島康三の作品の全側面を賞賛し続けていた。彼と出会う人は皆、我を忘れて野島について語るハナヤ氏の姿に、深い感動を覚えずにはいられなかった。彼は、日本のアマチュアやプロの写真家たちの作品を、できるだけ多くの人々の目に触れる機会を作るために努力を重ねていた。その努力は1980年代になってようやく、彼の写真仲間たちの作品が美術館で紹介され始めることで実を結びつつあった。この野島康三展の開催はハナヤ氏の長年の夢であった。しかし展覧会開催の二カ月前に、ハナヤ氏は永久に帰らぬ人となってしまった。

以下の小論は野島康三とその作品に対する私の賛歌であり、美術という普遍的な言語を通じて、野島の業績が世界人々に理解されることを心から願うものである。

野島は1889年2月12日、埼玉県浦和市に生まれた。彼の家は何代も続いた旧家であり、父親は中井銀行頭取であった。資料によれば、野島家の系図は西暦1700年頃まで遡ることができ、徳川幕府の御用商人を務めた商家であった。経済的に豊かであった野島家は、鎌倉の大仏で有名な浄土宗本山高徳院の有力な檀家の一つであり、野島康三も彼の先祖もこの寺で修行をしている。野島家の物質的豊かさと社会的地位の高さが、彼が作品の制作や芸術に対する支援を続ける上で、大きな助けとなったことは間違いない。

野島は1905年から1912年の期間、慶応義塾に通っている。慶応義塾は1867年、近代化を急いだ明治期の指導的な知識人の一人である福沢諭吉によって創立され、第一級の人文学系の私立大学として今日まで続いている。野島が学んだ当時の教授たちは、明治期の学者の最終世代に当る。彼らは西洋の思想体系を詳細に研究し、それらを日本の価値体系の文脈の中に統合する作業を進めていた。彼らの多くは海外に留学し、帰国後は、文明開化という国策を推進し運営するために雇用されていた外国人御用学者たちから、その地位を引き継いでいった。ここで、日本の明治期に起きた出来事の本質、すなわち、「日本は1853年のペリー提督の浦賀来航以後、単に受動的な西洋化を受け入れていたのではなく、近代社会を求めて自ら積極的にその歴史を変革した」(＊1)という事実を理解しておくことは極めて重要である。日本は自発的かつ積極的に、物質文明とともに様々な西欧の思想を輸入し、土着化あるいは共存化という経過を経て、次第にそれらを自己のものとして取り入れて行ったのである。野島とその仲間達は、自己抑制、自己の確立、人道的行動規範などを基調とする西欧式の大学教育を受けた最初の世代と言われている。また、野島が学生であった頃は、日本の芸術の分野でもこれらの思想がより深化され、同時代の問題として意識され始めた時であった。

19世紀の産業や科学思想の展開にともない、リアリズムはヨーロッパ芸術における中心的な論点となっていた。しかし、当時の日本でリアリズムは、芸術における様式的・思想的問題として明確には認識されていなかった。1861年まで、日本には西洋美術を研究する公的な機関はなく、そうした機関が設立された後も、リアリズムは有効な潜在的可能性を持つもう一つの技術という認識が強かった。1857年、横浜と北海道の函館に新たに外国人居住区が設けられ、日本の芸術家たちも様々な芸術的技能を持つ外国人と接する機会が多くなった。例えば、飯沢耕太郎氏の調査によれば、画家の高橋由一は1863年に、イギリス人特派員である挿図画家のチャールズ・ワーグマンを横浜に訪ね、思いがけずそこで、ワーグマンのパートナーである写真家のフェリーチェ・ビアトーに出会ったという。高橋由一は独学で西洋式の油絵を描き始め、司馬江漢の書物を再発見して感動し、絵画を通じて〈真実〉の追求にその生涯を捧げた画家であった。高橋由一は、絵画における〈真実〉の表現は、写実表現の技術以上のものであることを認識した最初の日本人画家として、日本美術史上きわめて重要な画家である。高橋由一にとって、真理の表現は芸術の本質的要素であった。

写真技術は、1839年にフランス人画家ルイ・ジャック・マンデ・ダゲールと、イギリス人科学者ウィリアム・ヘンリー・フォックス・タルボットの二人によって、全く同時期に別々に、異なる二つの方法が発明されたとされている。写真時代の始まりを告げるこの発明は、機械工学や化学、産業の成熟という状況から必然的に生まれたものと言える。同時にこの発明は、19世紀に一般化した科学的・分析的思考や、リアリズムという時代的美意識を如実に反映した結果であるとも言えるであろう。

初めて写真機が日本に渡来したのは1848年であった。それは長崎の出島という日本が西洋に向けて開いていた小さな入口から、様々な近代の物品に混じって輸入されてきたのである。出島から渡来するこれら西欧の知識と技術は、日本における近代産業と科学の定着と発展に先駆的な役割を果たした。物理的技術による新しい世界認識を人々にもたらし、〈真実を表現〉する写真術は、日本語で、「真実を写すもの」という言葉が与えられた。この日本語の語方は、今日でも〈フォトグラフィー（写真）〉を指す言語記号としてきわめて有効なものである。

写実小説と自然主義の運動が、近代日本文学の初期に作家や評論家によって創り出された。彼らは観察できる現象を尊重し、五感で知覚できる現実に注目したのである。主要な新聞紙上で毎日発表される彼らの作品は、同時代の日本人の生活にある視覚的側面を形成していった。当時最も読まれ、影響力のあった作家は、夏目漱石であった。彼の作品、『草枕』(1906)の主要登場人物は、自立した女性と近代様式を求める画家であった。彼らの会話によって漱石は、芸術家の姿に託して近代社会の入口に立つ日本の様子を描いている。『三四郎』(1908)では主人公である地方出身の青年が、東京大学に入り、都会のインテリ層や初恋に出会う様子が描かれている。この小説で漱石は、詩と絵画の時間と表現の限界におけるメディアの違いについての非常に近代的な論争を展開している。この論点は、ゴットールド・エフレム・レッシングの『ラオコーン:絵画と詩の限界について』の中の主題ときわめて共通するものであり、漱石の作品は、西欧思想からの洗練された援用以上のものがある。彼の新しい文学の中では、芸術制作は近代の意識を表現する方法として議論され、自我の確立やそれに伴う疎外についても考察されている。

若い作家や知識人たちの新しい波は、個人の自己表現を推賞し、この運動を通して個人は近代の主人公として明確に意識され始めたのである。こうした状況の中で、野島康三は真摯に芸術に傾倒し、真剣に西洋絵画を試み、最初の写真を撮り始めていったのである。

1907年、野島康三は、絵画主義写真の研究・制作のために発足した東京写真研究会(1907-)に、自分の作品を送っている。1904年から1909年の間、同研究会の最初の会長を務めた秋山轍輔(1888-1944)は、海外の写真に関する出版物を翻訳し、西洋の絵画主義写真家たちの間で用いられていた様々なピグメント印画の工程を紹介した。(*2) 東京写真研究会は、日本で最初の写真材料の製造、輸入、流通業者の一つであった小西六の援助を受けていた。この頃までに写真機材や材料は、量産され、一般の人々にも簡単に入手できるようになり、一挙に写真は個人のレヴェルに普及していった。19世紀の写真のほとんど全てが、商業写真館で撮影されていたことを考えると、これはきわめて大きな変化であったと言うことができる。個人で撮影できる写真術が普及することで、余暇として絵を描くことを考えていたアマチュア美術家たちが写真に目を向け始め、その中から、真剣に芸術としての写真を目指す人々が出現してきた。

野島康三の初期の作品は、当時の絵画主義写真の指導的サロンであった東京写真研究会の年次展覧会に出品されて大きな注目を集め、賞賛され、野島は新進の写真家として認知されていった。このような写真サロン活動は、パリのフォト・クラブ、英国のリンクド・リング、アメリカのフォト・セセションの展開とも類似したものであった。黒田清輝が審査員の一人を務めた(*3)1911年の第二回展では、野島の出品作《にごれる海》(1910,pl.1)は、第二

席を受賞している。この作品の内容も目標も、当時の日本の画家たちの間の主流であった外光派の手法を手本としている。しかしこの作品はまた、リアリズムからより主観的な芸術表現への移行を窺わせるものでもあった。野島は、写真の技術を修得しその歴史を理解していく過程で、自分が選んだこの写真という新しい表現メディアは、自分の作家としての成長とともに深化され、発展されうるものと考えていた。彼が抱いたこの批評的感覚は、当時台頭していた他の画家たちと野島が共有する経験であった。自己表現という目標で結ばれた野島と同時代の画家たちとの絆は、この日本の文化と思想の中に成長していた新しい理念によって影響を受け、支持されていたものであった。

ここでもう一度、明治時代の大変革の本質が、「この変革は西洋の思想の受容に繋がる単なる文化的模倣や知的好奇心ではなく、重大な心理的不安のなかでの、知的秩序に対する日本人の強い欲求であった」(*4)ということを認識しておく必用がある。野島の大学生時代には西欧の理念はなお、過去の寸断された歴史の参照や再構築、あるいは日露戦争(1904-1905)や韓国併合(1910)に対する政治・軍事的独走に対する批評的役割を果たしていた。20世紀に入り日本は産業経済国家への変革と移行を完了したが、野島康三と同時代の人々は、国際的な文脈の中で自己のアイデンティティを確立することに苦闘していた。大正時代の初めまでに、日本の第一次近代化運動のエネルギーは沈静化していた。次第に強まる保守主義の中で、人々は国家への忠誠心と、近代社会における日本の未来に対する疑問を内在化し始めていた。彼らは自分たちの生活や才能を犠牲にして、彼らの理想の実現と個人の真実を求めて、ますます強まる官僚主義に対し勇気をもって抵抗していったのである。

大正時代に入ると、文部省主催の文展の洋画部門では、審査員の期待から大きく逸脱する作品が増加していた。新しい世代の作家たちは彼らの作品を、フュウザン会(1912-1913)、二科会(1914-)、草土社(1915-21)、創作版画協会(1918-)などの文展とは独立した場で発表し始めていた。彼らは積極的に、後期印象派、表現主義、フォーヴィズム、立体主義や非具象絵画などの様々な様式の折衷と実験を試みていた。岸田劉生、梅原龍三郎、萬鐵五郎、中川一政ら野島と親しく交流した画家たちは、これらの展覧会に参加し、その組織の創立者であり主要メンバーであった。

彼らの活動は、おもに東京の神田を中心としていた。当時この古い町の一角は、今日以上に出版社や書店、古本屋が軒を並べていた。文筆家たちにとって神田は、ちょうどニューヨークのグリニッジ・ヴィレッジのように居心地のよい雰囲気の地域であった。彫刻家であり評論家でもある高村光太郎は1910年にヨーロッパから帰国し、神田の近くの淡路町に「瑯玕堂」という画廊を開いていた。黒田清輝に学んだ岸田劉生は黒田から決別する前の1912年4月、この画廊で個展を開いている。東京写真研究会の中で、小野隆太郎、

山崎静村、山本義雄らと〈四人会〉を結成していた野島康三は、高村光太郎の画廊をしばしば訪れている。1908年から1903年までパリに留学し、ルノアールにと接する機会を得た梅原龍三郎は、帰国後すぐ、1913年10月5日から14日まで神田近くの三崎町のヴィーナ・スクラブで展覧会を開いている。岸田劉生は10月の16日から22日までここで展覧会を開催し、1914年3月には銀座近くの尾張町の三笠画廊でも展覧会を開いた。(＊5)

当時の野島の活動についての資料は乏しいが、1909年の東京写真研究会主催の第二回写真品評展に彼の作品が出品されている。野島は1910年の東京写真研究会の第一回展にも出品しているが、1911年には健康を害し慶応義塾大学を中退した。しかし家族からの援助を受けながら、野島は写真と美術の活動を続けた。現存する当時の作品の数は少ないが、すでに、後に彼の作品の特徴となる優れた印画技術と明確で真剣な意思の統合をその作品から窺うことができる。1915年、野島康三は神田近くの人形町に三笠写真店を開設する。野島はそこに自分専用のスタジオを持ち、写真と同時に絵画の研究も進め、助手とともに肖像写真の注文制作を行なっていた。同年、野島は写実主義の詩人であった正岡子規が創設した謡会のメンバーとなった。この会には、子規の親友の夏目漱石や、河東碧梧桐、高浜虚子なども参加していた。彼らはしばしば野島の自宅に集い、論議を交わしていた。

この時代の芸術思潮は、新しい芸術のための雑誌である『白樺』(1941-23)の強い影響下にあった。彼らの芸術主張は極端な自然主義であり、そこでは個人主義や芸術における完全なる自由が常に唱えられていた。『白樺』の創刊当時、その主要な執筆者たちの多くはまだ学習院の学生であった。彼らはセザンヌやマチスなどの画家たちを書物から学び、翻訳し、出版した。後には、ヴァン・ゴッホやロダンから、東京の当時の様子、15世紀イタリア美術にまで及ぶ、包括的な美術史を紹介し始めた。当時の美術史の実践はまだ初歩的なものであり、これが当時の美術史に与えた具体的な影響を明確に判断することはできない。また『白樺』は、多くの展覧会を主催して開催し、多数の評論も発行している。『白樺』の活動は、この時代に自己の個性を発見し表現することを求めた作家たちのロマンチックなイメージを基調にしていたが、実は、近代リアリストの活動に鋭く焦点を当てていたのであり、それが野島康三に個人の真実の高潔さを伝えたのであろう。

野島は彼の作品の制作を続けながら経験を重ね、同時代の芸術家たちとの交流を広げていった。1919年6月からの1年間、野島は神保町の交差点近くに、兜屋畫画堂を開設した。兜屋畫堂はギャラリーであり、人の集うところであった。この畫堂では、フュウザン会、二科会、日本創作版画協会、草土社などの画家たちの作品が定期的に展示され、また、当時活躍していた日本の新進作家たちの作品も見ることができた。兜屋畫堂の最も重要な成果は、たぶんこ

れら多岐に渡る作家たちの作品を一同に集め、作家たちが公的な場で、互いの作品を鑑賞し尊敬しあう機会を創り出したことであろう。兜屋畫堂は商業的な画廊ではなく、実験と研鑽の場であった。野島は常にこの畫堂に現れ、収集し、芸術鑑賞の目を養い、多くの友人を得ていったのである。兜屋畫堂は小さな規模であったが、一般の人々が生活の場にとけ込んだ場で、日本の近代美術の展覧会を見られる重要な場所であった。

1920年に閉鎖された兜屋畫堂の活動の後も、野島は引続き彼の広い自邸のサロンを解放し、陶芸家の富本憲吉、画家の岸田劉生、萬鐵五郎、梅原龍三郎らの美術史的にも批評的にもきわめて重要な作品展を開催していった。彼が組織した展覧会に対する当時の膨大な批評文や、作家たちから彼に寄せられた私信の山からも、彼の努力がいかに重要なものであったかがわかる。兜屋畫堂や野島邸で展示された作品の多くが、日本近代美術の上で重要なキー・ストーンになっていると言えるだろう。また野島は、日本の近代美術の主要な組織創りにも設立メンバーの一人として重要な役割を果たしている。それらには、フュウザン会、草土社、二科会のメンバーを統合した春陽会(1922-)や、後に、国画会(1928-)になる国画創作協会(1925-26)の洋画部門がある。これらの組織の定例展覧会に、野島は自分の油彩画を出品している。

『白樺』、『中央美術』などの美術誌は兜屋畫堂が開催する展覧会に大きな注目を払っていた。このカタログ中の光田由里氏の論考の中では、兜屋畫堂の展覧会記録が詳細に調査され、記述されている。兜屋畫堂の活動が、野島康三の写真という文脈からこれほど詳しく調査されたのは初めてであり、今後の日本美術史の研究の上でも貴重なものとなるであろう。日本の近代美術史研究の主流は兜屋畫堂の活動を見落としてきたが、歴史上の事実や出来事を再収集し、再構成する作業は常に重要である。兜屋畫堂で、写真作品が展示されたかどうかは手元の資料では解らないが、たぶん写真は展示されなかったと思われる。写真を美術展として開催することは、1920年の日本ではまだ早すぎたと言わざるを得ない。芸術写真の個人収集家たちの市場はまだ成立しておらず、芸術写真家たちの職業としての仕事の機会もほとんど存在しなかった。彼らの立場では芸術写真の制作では、職業として経済的に自立することは不可能であり、その活動の場はアマチュア活動という枠内に留まるものであった。「アマチュアリズムは個人の意識の全的な覚醒と、社会の批評的基盤の発展を求める。」(＊6)　この点において野島はアウトサイダーであり、公的な文化活動の枠組みの外で活動する機会をすばやく掴んでいたと言えるだろう。すなわちそれは自由な立場を守ろうとする感覚であり、そのことはまた、彼の創造力の発揚の基盤がどこにあったかを明確に証明していることになるだろう。

1920年に野島康三は、東京写真研究会の第10回研展の会場で小規模な回顧展を開催しいる。山崎静村は展覧会評の中で次のような分析を行なっている。

1907年に最初の作品を東京写真研究会に出品してから、兜屋画堂のオープンまで、野島の写真にたいするアプローチと哲学は、三つの段階を経て発展している。最初は〈無意識の時代〉である:物の見方をトレーニングし、意味の表現方法と自分独自の行き方を模索する、ガム・プリントの手法を使い、完成した写真により多くの作者の作意を込めようとした。ガム・プリントは手作業に向く技法であり、作者の印画の制御が構成の中で重要な場合や、意識的に主観的な表現の作品には、最も人気のある技法であった。野島は熟考の過程で、人それぞれの目で事物を見るべきであり、伝統や外部の規範によって見るべきではないこと本能的に理解するようになった。こう確信するようになる過程で、彼は文学の自然主義に影響を受け、自然な感情で仕事を進め、写真の中にその感情を表現しようとした。

野島の成長の第二段階は〈絵画主義写真〉である。彼は絵画表現をより深く知り、実際にその経験を積むために絵画の研究に以前より力を注いだ。また日本の伝統的美術の様々な面も発見していった。彼は慎重にゆっくりと何ヵ月もかけて一枚のネガから最高のプリントを制作していった。野島はガム・プリント技術を展開し、染料を選択的に付与できるブロムオイル・プリントを試し始めた。《M氏の肖像》(1917、pl.12)は、この最高の例である。ブロムオイル・プリントの色調やブラシの使用は、野島の画家的本能を満足させるものであった。以前は部分にこだわっていた野島は、全体を統一された絵画空間として見るようになった。これは大きな前進であった。絵画主義の時期の初めに、野島は三笠写真店を開いている。

野島が兜屋畫堂を開いた1919年までに、絵画的表現の広範囲な研究と真理の探求は、絵画的写真と現実の印画作品の最終的な特質との間の避けられない矛盾の袋小路にさしかかっていた。野島は数カ月間にわたって作品の制作を止め、兜屋畫堂に展示していた絵画作品をあらためて研究し直していった。やがて野島康三は、光・影・形態、そして写真メディア特有のモデリング・ライトの造形的特質に注目したのである。野島の作品が持つヴィジョンの力は、一つには卓抜した手仕事による質の高い印画に負うところが大きい。飯沢耕太郎氏が指摘するように、野島の1920年代の肖像写真は、強い存在感に溢れている。

1920年に兜屋畫堂を閉鎖した後、野島は三笠写真店を売却し、スタジオを神田から九段に移し、野々宮写真館を開設した。野々宮という名前は能の演題から引用されたものであった。野々宮写真館は皇居の北側に位置し、その後23年間に渡って運営され、肖像写真と高い技術サービスでよく知られていた。1923年の関東大震災のあと、野々宮写真館は、フランク・ロイド・ライトに学んだ建築家・土浦亀城の設計による美しい近代的な建物に新築され、再びこの町に姿を現わした。新しい野々宮ビルは、インターナショナル・スタイルで建設された東京で初めてのアパート・ホテルであり、野々宮写真館はこの一階に設けられていた。そして野々宮写真館は、近代写真運動の台頭期に多くの若い写真家たちが野島の助言や励ましを求めて集まる場所でもあった。

当時日本に入ってきた新しい思想の流入経路や分散の様について、確実にその経過を辿ることは困難である。野島康三は彼が感じ取ったこうした影響などについて、何の記録も日記も残してはいない。彼が残した蔵書の中には、戦前発行のアメリカやイギリス、ドイツの写真関係の出版物があった。彼はまた『アルス』や『アサヒカメラ』、『写真月報』などの日本の写真雑誌に寄稿し、その編集者や評論家たちとも親しく交流していた。これらの雑誌は10年代から20年代初めにかけて、日本の芸術写真運動を擁護し、20年代後半から第二次世界大戦の始まりまでは近代写真の運動を取りあげていた。1931年、朝日新聞社はドイツのシュトゥッガルトで開催された「映画と写真展」から再構成した、「独逸国際移動写真展」の日本巡回展を実現した。この展覧会は世界の近代写真の動向=新しい写真のメッセージを伝えるものであった。まさにこの時期、芦屋出身の写真家、中山岩太とハナヤ勘兵衛らは〈芦屋カメラ倶楽部〉(1930-1941)の第二回展覧会を東京で開いていた。これらの動向によって、日本にもアヴァンギャルドの写真家が現れ始めているという新しい認識が広まっていた。

「独逸移動写真展」の一年後、野島は日本の近代写真運動のメッセージを広く伝えるために、新しい出版物を発行する必要性を感じ、自己資金をつぎ込んで『光画』を創刊した。野々宮写真館を拠点に、野島は『光画』の主要メンバーとして写真家の中山岩太や木村伊兵衛、評論家の伊奈信男を結集し、これに、バウハウスに学んだグラフィック・デザイナーの原弘が加わった。彼らは定期的に『光画』に寄稿し、レイアウトなどの編集作業にも参加した。『光画』は1932年5月から1933年10月まで継続し、全18巻が発行された。この間『光画』のメンバーたちは、写真の新しい方向を支え発展させるために精力的に活動し、当時の日本で撮影・制作された最高水準の写真を同誌に収録していった。海外文献の翻訳と写真に関する論説も各号に掲載され、国内外の写真の展開が日本で最初の専門的な写真評論家、板垣高穂と伊奈信男の二人によって分析された。彼らのヨーロッパのアヴァンギャルド写真に対する扱いは包括的で多岐にわたり、また、『光画』の第一巻の見開きに掲載された伊奈信男の宣言「写真に帰れ」は、写真に対する新しい視点と、真の写真の成立を宣言するものであった。

1933年に野島康三と原弘は協力して、写真展の一つの実験的なモデルの提案としての、「野島康三作、写真・女の顔20点」を開催した。この展覧会は当時の有力画廊の一つであった東京銀座にある紀ノ国屋ギャラリーで行なわれた。この時まで写真の展覧会は多くの場合、絵画展と同じ形式での展示か、もしくは旅行や販売促進というテーマ・ショウの規模を超えるものではなかった。野島と原は、従来のアプローチは彼らの新しい芸術の追求にとっては否定的な意味しかないと考えていた。野島は20枚の559×457 mmのゼラチンシルバー・プリントによる女性の顔の拡大写真を制作し、原に、これらの作品はガラス無しで展示し、説明パネルも展覧会場のどこ

か目だたぬ所に取り付けたいとだけ依頼した。この依頼を受けて原は、写真を会場の部屋を巡る白く塗られた薄いパネルの上に当間隔で配置するデザインを考え出した。出品された《女の顔》の作品は大胆にトリミングされた写真であり、前年に制作された野島のブロムオイルによる肖像写真とは明確に区別できるものであった。実際の人間の二倍に引き延ばされ、ストレートな女の頭部の写真は、冷たいグレーの壁に据付けられた白いパネルの帯に取り付けられ、強烈な照明の下でダイナミックな視覚的効果を生みだしていた。あたかも野島が『ヴォーグ』のファッションやその語法を援用し、新しい女性像を記録し、東京という近代都市の環境に、彼の新しい眼差しを向けたかのようであった。明らかにこの時期の野島は、以前彼が熱中していたピグメント印画による技術的熟練を捨て、彼の作品をゼラチンシルバー・プリントという新しい技法の中に再編成しようとしていたように思われる。

野島は他の試みもいくつか続けたが、『光画』が廃刊になる1933年頃には、日本の近代写真の活動はあきらかにその継続が困難になり始めた。国内にファシズムが台頭し、国家および地方の権力は、前衛芸術家たちを無政府主義者もしくは破壊活動を助長する不穏分子と見なしていた。1938年、野島は国画会に写真部門を創設し、1940年の同会の展覧会に忘れ難い一組のフォトグラムを出品した(pl.103)。1941年、多くの芸術家や写真家たちが国家への忠誠を誓い、喜んで当局の戦争広告や宣伝に参加し始めたが、野島康三はこの圧力に対して朝日カメラの6月号に次のような文を寄稿した。「誰も自分の満足する芸術を行なうかどうかを決める権利を持つ。もしそれがやりたいことであれば報道写真を撮ることもできるが、私は報道写真を撮らないことを選ぶ。」これが野島と日本の近代写真の運動メンバーとの精神的な決別であった。(＊8)

近代のフォーマリズムや様式主義は野島の主要関心事ではなかった。彼の感性や美に対する目は事物の表面深くに据えられ、野島は彼自身の感性と自己認識に対し穏やかな自信を持っていた。野島の持つこの資質が最も有効に開花したのは、1930年に制作された静物、《仏手柑》(pl.28)という作品においてであろう。日本の他の芸術家たちが自己の知覚に忠実な表現形式を求めながら、そこに自己のアイデンティティーを確立することに失敗した中で、野島康三はこの作品によって、彼が求めていた内的調和を成し遂げたのである。他の芸術家たちにとってこの危機は、時として極端な解決法を招いていた。白樺派の作家の幾人かは自殺を実行し、伝統や保守的な画壇という組織に回帰するものも少なくなかった。あるいは海外への逃避も、その解答の一つであった。ごく僅かな芸術家たちだけが、この根源的な問題意識を持続させ、近代運動の基本問題に留まり続けたのであった。

戦前の日本の前衛写真と近代写真の動向は、1930年代前半までその実験的な活力を維持していた。しかし、やがてその活力と才能

は、広告や出版という商業写真の領域へと吸収されていく。第二次大戦後、出版界は大きく繁栄したが、野島の写真作品はこの恩恵には浴さなかった。戦後の混乱の中で野島の健康は悪化し、財政的にも困難な状況を迎えた野島は、鎌倉近郊へ隠遁し、その晩年を静かに過ごしていった。

ごく近い過去を検証し、既成の理解を再編成することを志す芸術家や美術史家たちが、野島康三の作品とその業績を再発見したのは、ごく最近のことであった。激動した時代に同時代精神のフロンティアに位置し続けた野島康三の精神には、芸術家の役割に対する普遍主義者としての次のような信念が常に持続されていたに違いない。

人々に喜びを與へ、感動を與へることができれば作者としては生き甲斐があったのだ。人間としての役割を立派につとめてゐるのだ。たとへ姓名、傳記は不明でも作者の心は作品に宿って此世に生きてゐるのだ。誰でもよい。いい作品を生んで貰ひたいものだ。(＊9)
訳:河本信治

註：
（1）『日本:前史時代から現代まで』、ジョン・ウイットニー・ホール著、デラコート・プレス、ニューヨーク、1970、pp.243.引用文は次の文章の後に続く:「日本の西洋との葛藤は、かつての中国文明との出会いと同じく日本の歴史に大きな転換点をもたらした。しかし、日本が外国の影響に単に圧倒されていたという一般の理解は、少なくとも19世紀の場合はあてはまらない。」
（2）ガム・プリントは、1895年頃からロバート・デマシーによって紹介され、人気の高かったパリのフォト・クラブでの展覧会や出版物によって国際的に普及していった。野島が用いた他のピグメント印画法としては、1895年にイギリス人トーマス・マンレーによって発明されたオブブロム・プリント;1905年イギリスで開発されたブロムオイル・プリントがある。（本図録の写真技法解説を参照）
（3）黒田清輝(1866-1924)、「東京写真研究会第二回展」、写真月報、1911
（4）「日本近代日本政治の知的基盤」、ナリタ・テツオ著、フェニックス、シカゴ大学出版局、1980、pp.86
（5）『芸美』1983年5月号によれば、三笠画廊は1914年1月―1915年6月の間活動した。これらの画家達については高階秀治の包括的な論考がある。「日本の中のパリ、背日本人とヨーロッパ絵画の出会い」展カタログ、セントルイス・ワシントン大学ほかアメリカ国内を巡回、国際交流基金、1987
（6）『メディアはメッセージである』、マーシャル・マックルーハン著、ニューヨーク、バンタム・ブック、1967、pp.93
（7）山崎静村、「野島康三氏の作品について」、写真月報、1920年4月号、PP.246-253
（8）野島の重要なこの言葉は、『現代日本写真全集』、第四巻、集英社、1978、に収録された重森弘淹氏の論文から引用した。
（9）野島康三、「人物作畫方」、アルス写真大講座第二巻、アルス社、1929

＊この小論は、1986年ポンピドゥ・センター、国立近代美術館で開催された〈前衛の日本:1910-1970〉展カタログに掲載された著者のフランス語論文「野島とアヴァンギャルド」を基礎に改筆したものである。

＊長年に渡り、多項目に及ぶ私の調査にご協力を頂いた野島康三遺作保存会に心から感謝の意を表する。また、野島康三の活動歴に関する私の調査は、飯沢耕太郎氏の助力に負うところが多かった。飯沢氏の膨大な著作は、野島の時代を研究する上での基本資料となっている。私の調査のために、資料翻訳の労を厭わず辛抱強く協力していただいた方々に心から感謝したい。誤解や解釈の誤りは、私の責任に帰されるべきものである。最後に、絶えず私を支えてくれた私の家族にも、心から感謝したい。

野島康三の"肖像"

飯沢耕太郎

もう20年近く前になるだろうか。野島康三の写真をはじめて見た時の印象を、まざまざと思い起こすことがある。

オリジナル・プリントではなく、『日本写真史／1840—1945』（平凡社、1971）に収録された写真図版だった。その「芸術写真」のパートに《樹による女》（1915、pl. 5）、《枇杷》（1930、pl.32）、「展開期」のパートに《細川ちか子氏》（1932、pl. 75）、《千田是也氏》（1932、pl. 76）、さらに "モデルF" のシリーズをはじめとする1931—33年に撮影された女性・ヌード写真がおさめられていた。

その印象を一言でいえば、比類のない強さということになるだろう。他の写真家たちの作品と比較して、野島の写真の存在感はきわだっていた。大地を踏みしめて立つ女たちの存在の確かさ、こちらを凝視する眼差しの強さは、一度見たら忘れられない強烈な印象だった。この写真集ではじめて見た安井仲治の写真の鋭利な現実感や、中山岩太の華麗な幻想世界もそれぞれ魅力的だったが、なんといっても野島康三の名前が脳裏に刻みこまれてしまった。

その後、しばらくシカゴ美術館に寄託されていた野島のプリントが日本に帰ってきて、いくつかの展覧会で実際に目にする機会があった。そのたびに、印刷物ではとうてい味わえない、なまなましい迫力を感じ続けてきた。その強さの秘密に迫ろうとして、〈大正の質感〉（『大正感情史』日本書籍、1979）をはじめとして、幾つかの野島論を書いてみたりもした。しかし、まだその全体をとらえきったとはとても思えない。これからも展覧会や出版などを機会として、野島に対して、畏怖とオマージュとが混じりあった思いを投げかけ続けていくのではないかと思う。

野島の写真の本質が、その肖像写真（ポートレイト）に凝縮していることは、否定できないだろう。彼には岸田劉生のいう「物質に対する愛」（〈写実論〉1920）をそのまま体現したような見事な静物写真があるし、軽井沢などの繊細な風景写真も忘れがたい。しかし量的にも、表現の質や厚みにおいても、肖像が圧倒的であることは間違いない。

のみならず、野島の肖像写真は日本の近代写真史においても、きわめて特異な位置を占めている。日本の写真家たちが、写真を意識的に "表現" の手段として用いはじめるのは、明治30年代（1900年前後）に「芸術写真」の理念が確立してからのことである。ゆふつづ社（創設1904年）や浪華写真倶楽部（同）の会員に代表されるアマチュア写真家たちは、「画其ものを唯一の目的物」（むらさき〈空蟬（一）〉1904）とするような「芸術写真」を求めて、技巧を競いあった。

その時、彼らによって徹底的に攻撃されたのが、営業写真館の写真家たちの型にはまった肖像写真であった。当時、写真を撮られること自体が恐れと驚きの対象だった時代は既に過ぎ去り、撮影行為は人々の生活にすっかり溶けこんでいた。当然、写真草創期の緊張感や創造性は薄れ、写真師たちはきまりきった背景で、同じようなポーズをとる肖像写真を大量生産していた。アマチュア写真家たちは、その「芸術思想」のなさを批判し、風景写真に活路を見出そうとした。肖像写真が、旧式な写真の代表と見なされた時期が

あったのである。

芸術写真家たちが風景写真を好んだ理由はそれだけではない。これは彼らが写真を業としないアマチュアであったことの限界でもあるのだが、多くの場合、写真は彼らによって手軽な趣味として選びとられていた。「芸術写真」を標榜してはいたが、自己や他者を厳しく見据え、美の理想や存在の意味を探るような真剣な取り組みは、ごく一部の作家を除いては見ることができなかった。むしろ、写真は手近な慰めであり、"近代生活" で傷ついた自我を優しく包みこむような場所でなければならなかった。「芸術写真」の作例にくりかえし出現する、輪郭を失い、背景に溶けこんでしまったような、ソフトフォーカスの水辺の風景は、アマチュア写真家のつかのまの安らぎの感情を投影したものではなかっただろうか。

こうしてみると、野島の肖像写真の自己と他者を見つめる凝視力の強さは、他に類のないものであることがわかる。写真は彼にとって趣味などというものではなく、時には自分自身を食い破りかねない、本気になって取り組まねばならない目標であった。彼の作品が、時に美的であるよりも倫理的に見えてくるのはそのためでもあろう。

野島の肖像写真を眺めていると、彼の同時代人よりも幕末・明治初期に活動した写真家や洋画家、たとえば横山松三郎や高橋由一の仕事が重なってくることがある。写真術が日本に入ってきた1850年代においては、洋画との区別はほとんど意識されていなかった。どちらも、その迫真的な「写実」の能力において、日本人を打ちのめした。横山は上野池之端に写真館とともに洋画塾、通天楼を経営していたし、高橋には風景写真の構図をそっくりそのまま借用した作品がある。彼らは写真と洋画の区別を超えて、眼前の事物をこれ以上ないほどリアルに写しとる "鏡" の出現に、文字通り夢中になってのめりこんでいったのである。

その "鏡" は彼らの周囲に広がる世界だけでなく、自分自身の姿も映し出していた。くっきりとした手ごたえと奥行きを備えた自己、あるいは内面の所在が、洋画や写真のような新しい "鏡" の登場によって、ありありと浮かびあがってきたのである。横山にも高橋にも自画像が知られている。特に横山は青年時代から晩年まで、写真と洋画の両方で、飽くことなくセルフポートレイトを制作し続けた。自己の発見は他者の認知につながる。自己から発した視線が他者に届き、その輪郭をまさぐり、自分とは異質な存在を自己表現の一部として取りこんでいくような、近代的な "肖像" の理念が少しずつ成長していくのである。

野島は幕末・明治の先駆者たちが実践した "肖像" の成立への過程を、誠実にたどり直しているように思う。ちょうど岸田劉生が、後期印象派（ポスト・インプレッショニズム）の影響から脱して、写実の系譜を逆向きにたどっていったように、彼は時にあの幕末・明治初期の肖像写真に刻みつけられた、存在そのものへの出会いの驚きを、ふたたび取り戻すことをめざしていたようにも見える。野島の肖像写真を見ると、「その人が、そこにいる」という素朴な、だが原型的な実在感に打たれることがある。それが彼の写真の強さの秘密（それだけではないが）なのではないだろうか。

以前、野島の肖像写真について書いた時に、彼の写真には時代的に二つのピークがあると指摘したことがある（「凝視する精神——野島康三論」1986）。ひとつは1920—23（大正9—12）年頃、もうひとつは1930—33（昭和5—8）年頃である。この二つの時期では、彼の人物・肖像写真のスタイルが微妙に変化している。

大正時代の作品の大部分はゴム印画法によるもので、構図は静的で古典的な印象を与える。モデルはじっとこちらを見つめ、静かに、だがきっぱりと自己の存在を主張している。白樺派の文学者やその周辺の画家たちから強い影響を受けた彼にふさわしく、そこにはきまじめに「人格の表現」を追求しようとする姿勢が見られる。この時期の彼の文章中の表現を借りれば「写真によって自分の内部生活を営む」（〈朱雪雑記〉1920）ということである。結果として、この時期の彼の肖像写真は、その静まりかえった外見にもかかわらず、自他の個性が火花を散らして切り結ぶ、緊張感を漂わせたものとなった。

ところが昭和期になると、その倫理的といえるような姿勢に加えて、別な要素が彼をとらえるようになる。彼の唯一のまとまった肖像写真論である〈人物作画法〉（1927）に次のように書かれているような「明暗、形からくる感覚」、「造形の面白み」の魅力である。

> 私は肖像をつくるとき、その対象を適当な光を受くる位置においてまづながめる。そうして明暗、形を調べる。面白いなと思つたらすぐに写す。私はそのときにその人物の性格を写し出さうとか、殊更に特長をめつけ出して写さうとか思はない。明暗、形からくる感覚によつて写す。そこに面白味を見出すのである。……表情を主として、その表情より生まれる一種の気分を写し出さうとする方法もであらうが私には出来ない。私は造形の面白味の方により多く興味を感じる。とにかく感覚を主として仕事しなくてはいけないと思ふ。

モデルは「人格」よりも、フォルムやプロポーションの造形美によってとらえられる。モデルから引き出される「明暗、形からくる感覚」が、〝肖像〟の構図や内容を決定するのである。大正時代の顔を中心とした安定した構図、どっしりとした重みある実在感は失われ、軽やかな感覚のひらめきがそのまま定着される。画面はよりダイナミックになり、顔をまっぷたつに切った構図（《細川ちか子氏》（pl. 75））や多重露光モンタージュのような大胆な実験も試みられるようになる。

このような〝肖像〟のスタイルの変化に、1930年代のいわゆる「新興写真」の影響があったことは間違いないだろう。野島ほど「ドイツにはじまった新しい写真運動」（木村伊兵衛）を誠実に受けとめた写真家はほかにいない。「感覚」の追求の結果として、きらびやかだが、ほとんど空疎なファッション写真風の作品すら、この時期の野島は制作している。しかし、その最も良質の部分は、『光画』（1932—33）に発表され、個展「写真女の顔・20点」（銀座、紀伊国屋ギャラリー、1933）に展示された、クローズアップの〝女〟の肖像に結実していくのである。

今回、野島の肖像写真をあらためて見直してみて、「新興写真」の直接的な影響による造形的な要素以外に、大正時代と1930年代の作品には、ある決定的な違いが存在していることに気づいた。

それは、なぜこの時期に野島が〝女〟の撮影にのめりこんでいったかということとも関係がある。《千田是也氏》などのわずかな例外はあるものの、『光画』や「写真女の顔・20点」で発表された肖像写真の大部分は〝女〟、しかも無名の女性をモデルとしたものである。特に『光画』創刊号（1932年5月）の写真ページの最初に掲げられた作品《女》（1931、pl. 70）のモデルとなった女性（〝モデルF〟と称される）に対しては、野島は異様なほどの執着を見せる。顔を中心とした表情だけでなく、全身像、ヌードなど、驚くべき量の肖像写真が残されている。こちらを見据える強い視線、ふてぶてしいほどの野性味のある表情、その肉体のどっしりした重量感——〝モデルF〟はこの時期の野島の理想の女性像を体現していたとしか思えない。

無名の女性たちの、千変万化する表情や身振りを追った1930年代の写真群は、大正時代の男性中心の肖像と、きわだった対比を見せている。大正時代の野島の写真のモデルとなったのは、柳宗悦、中川一政、富本憲吉などの当時の一流の文化人（野島の親しい友人でもあった）であった。野島家の書生をモデルにした《S氏肖像》（1921、pl. 16）や《風邪の少年》（1920、pl. 13）など、無名の〝男〟の肖像もある。しかし、それでも男たちはある確固とした社会的地位を占め、名前と個性を備えた「人格」として撮影されている。

1930年代の女性写真のモデルたちは、反対に名前も「人格」も持たない。〝F〟という呼び名が象徴しているように、彼女たちは置きかえが可能な一種の記号である。大正時代の写真がほとんど一人のモデルにつき一点しか制作されていないのに対して、1930年代の〝女〟たちは、定点観測のようにくりかえし撮影されている。

関東大震災以前の大正時代と、1920—30年代の文化状況を分ける最も大きな違いは、近代的な都市の環境が成立したことではないかと思う。そのめまぐるしく変動する、多面的な空間を漂うのは、固定した〝顔〟を持つ個人ではなく、〝顔〟のない群衆—やがて〝顔〟を欠いたまま戦時体制に動員されていく—であった。野島の〝女〟たちは、まさにその都市の群衆のただ中からすくいあげられてきたように見える。彼女たちは、ヤナギ・ムネヨシやセンダ・コレヤといった固有の名前で呼ばれるよりは、〝F〟という記号によってさし示されるのにふさわしい存在であったのだ。

彼女たちが個人ではないからこそ、逆に1930年代という時代と、東京という場所がより強くその顔や身体に刻みこまれることになる。〝モデルF〟のふてぶてしさも、肉の重みも、あらゆる感情を包みこむようなその表情も、この時代と場所にすべて含みこまれていたものかもしれない。野島は驚くべき忍耐力で変幻する〝女〟のなかに踏みこみ、1930年代の東京——つかのまの近代都市（モダン・シティ）の輝きを、まるごと抱き寄せようとしているように見える。

もちろん都市の群衆のなかから〝モデルF〟を選びとった彼の眼は、比類のない独特のものである。考えてみれば、野島の女性・ヌード写真の最も初期の作品である《樹による女》（1915、pl. 5）から

彼の好みは見事に一貫している。力強く、大地に根をはやしたよう
な、まさに〝母なるもの〟の象徴としての女性のイメージを、彼はい
つでも求め続けていた。華やいだ近代都市（モダン・シテイ）の狂躁、表層の感覚を
波立たせるエロティシズムと、地母神を思わせる土の匂いのする女
性のイメージが、驚くべき強さで結びつけられる。野島の肖像写真
の最大の魅力は、一枚の写真のなかに、ちょうど積み重なった地層
のように、出自を異にするイメージが共存していることなのかもしれな
い。

残念なことに、彼の肖像写真があの忘れがたい魅力を発していた
時代は、それほど長くは続かなかった。病気がちだった彼の健康状
態が、作品制作への集中力を奪っていったし、戦時体制への移行
によって写真家たちの自由な創作活動は、1940年代にはほとんど不
可能になってしまった。野島は第二次大戦後の1964年まで生きる
が、晩年はほとんど見るべき作品を残していない。
〝肖像〟というジャンルそのものが解体しつくしてしまった現在、野島
の肖像写真はあまりにも古めかしく、時代遅れに見えるかもしれない。
だがなぜか彼の写真を見るたびに、奇妙なたかぶりと感動を覚え
る。厚みのないはずのイメージが、生気を取り戻し、なまなましく息づ
きはじめるのだ。野島の写真についての反応は見る人によって、また
時代によって違ってくるだろうが、「その人が、そこにいる」というあの
素朴な、だが最も原型的な実在感は、簡単に消えてなくなるようなも
のではないだろう。　　　　　　　（いいざわ・こうたろう／写真評論家）

野島康三の裸婦像をめぐって

光田由里

1―――野島康三の位置と《裸胸婦》

やや腰をひねって女は腕をあげ、《裸胸婦》（1930、pl. 45）のトルソが練り上がる。強くくびれた腰から、あやうくほどけんばかりに巻きついた下着の黒が、豊かに流れ落ちる黒髪の形と呼びあう。彼女の顔―目鼻立ちの複雑な造作―はシンプルなフォルムにとって替わり、官能が緊張している。無心な、強靱なからだ。左端の垂直の柱と、右端の障子の丸い引き手が、彼女の野生的なからだを狭い和室に閉じ込めて、まぎれもない日本の女の実質が、伝統ともモダンとも呼べない強固な美のうちに生かされている。
野島康三はここで、日本の女性のリアルな美を、緻密に焼き上げたブロムオイル・プリントの重厚な質感のなかに描き切っている。単純ながら緊迫した幾何学的な構成とヴォリュームに、近代的な野島の造形意識が結晶されている一方で、彼の表現しようとした「感覚の美」が、当時の日本の実質を洞察し肯定しようとする野島の精神力のために、質の高い表現へと結実されていることに気づかされる。
彼は写真機という伝来の機械を用い、絵画にはるかに下って生まれた写真という方法で、西欧化をいそぐ日本の近代に、独自の作品を生み出したのである。

洋画とほぼ同時期に日本にもたらされた写真は、もともと西洋の進んだ科学技術として研究されてきた。両者の目新しいリアルさは、日本では同じ様な驚きで受けとめられ、西洋の画家たちが写真の出現に畏怖と好奇をつのらせたような、両者の相剋は起きえなかった。それはまた、ヨーロッパでもそうであったような、写真は絵画という芸術とは違い、純粋な技術である、とする認識とも矛盾しなかった。近代の奇妙な状況の下で、日本の写真もやはり遅れてきた表現となったのである。写真が表現手段だと考えられ始めたのは、明治後期のことである。
営業写真家が純粋な技術者となる一方で、写真を表現手段として担っていったのは、高価な趣味である写真に凝ったアマチュアたちだった。彼らはサロン的な同好会を作った。野島が活躍した主な舞台である東京写真研究会もその最も古いもののひとつで、1907年に設立されている。
アマチュアたちがぎこちなく"表現"を始めた、そうした時期に野島も生きている。彼らが日本画・洋画を含めて、絵画に範を求めたのは当然のことだった。一般に「芸術写真」とよばれるそうした写真は、日本ではまず日本画的な情緒表現から始まっている。写真独自の表現ではないと非難されてきたそれらの作品に、簡便な借り物の美意識しかなければむろん批判されねばならないが、深い自然観照により魅力ある表現に達した写真家もいたのである。（＊1）ピグメント印画法を駆使した写真を、絵画の美学をとりいれたという理由だけで批判する、素朴な見方は現在は意味を失っている。それはドイツ流の新興写真を経て、報道写真へと重点を移していった、続く写真の展開の途上の、一時的な観点でしかないだろう。

野島康三は、卓抜した作家である。対象の実在を極めて深部でつかみ、伝統でも外来でもない独自の美学を求め、緻密な技術で高い精神性をたたえた表現に達した。彼は本展で比較されるように、岸田劉生、梅原龍三郎、萬鐵五郎、中川一政ら同時代の洋画の最良の部分を参照している。友人の洋画家たちに数年遅れながら、彼自身の表現を得てゆく野島は、開拓者ではなかったかもしれないが、実現者だったといってもよいだろう。

野島は写真の側から絵画を眺めたのではなく、絵画を絵画として見、写真を写真として見、同時代の美術を本質的に理解するすぐれた〈見る人〉であった。彼は岸田たちのパトロン、コレクターであったと同時に、展覧会企画、作品撮影を通して、それらを解釈しプロデュースしてゆくメディア的な存在でもあった。そのことは、彼の作品が持ち得た位置に直接関係している。

彼の中には、絵画／写真、西洋／日本、機械／表現といった、当時の様々な表現者の課題が、静かに融合された瞬間があったようにみえるのである。それは、写真の持つ受動的な性質が、すぐれた〈見る人〉としての野島（＊2）の性質と重なりあった、特異な幸運というべきなのだろうか。写真家・野島の視線は、"西洋"を常に摂取し解釈しようとし続けてきた日本近代の視線と重なりはしないだろうか。

これらの課題がもはや、課題として扱われることが少なくなってきたのは、解決されたからではないだろう。現在の写真をめぐる循環的な消費構造と入れ子状の虚構性のなかで、野島の作品がもつ独特の位置と精神性は極めて新鮮であり、イメージ力についての考察を可能にするはずである。

2───初期・裸婦像と《樹による女》

野島康三の実質的な制作期間は、75年の生涯の中でも短かったといわねばならない。しかも全作品が残されているわけではなく、彼の死後、259点が"発見"されたに過ぎない。それらの作品でしか判断することはできないにしても、特筆すべき作品が生まれたのはきわめて限られた時期でしかなく、1915—23年の初期と1930—33年なのである。両時期ともに、すぐれた裸婦像が目立って制作された。強靱な半裸像《裸胸婦》は1930年作だが、年記はプリント時のもので、撮影時はもっと遡るかもしれない。野島は撮影してから時間のたったフィルムを焼き付けることもしばしばあったし、1914年—23年の初期裸婦像の多くが、着物の胸をはだけ、下半身を覆った半裸像だからである。

《髪を梳く女》（1914, pl. 4）では、化粧する女の伝統的なポーズが採用されている。からだの表現を、陰影よりは、繊細にリタッチした輪郭線によっている点にも、いまだ浮世絵の色濃い影響をよみとることができる。《立てる女》（1917, pl. 7）など1920年までの裸婦のほとんどに、これと同じことがいえる。《女》（1918, pl. 8）の、太く作られた輪郭線と、ヴォリュームを押さえた表面的な描写は、まさしくこの時期までの野島が、日本画における美学とともにあったことを示している。

彼女たちは、化粧や着替えの際の日常的なポーズをとり、江戸時代までの伝統的な風俗画のなかの裸体にとどまっている。（＊3）無表情に目をそらした女たちは、無力なまま受け身で、撮影されていることを忘れようとさえしている。

しかし、上の範疇に入らない異色作がある。野島の代表作の一つ《樹による女》（1915, pl. 5）である。硬い輪郭線ではあるが、一本の樹の幹に手を置いて、地に足を踏みしめる野太い半裸の女が重厚に描写されている。この構図は、基本的には、インド起源で東西にあった樹下美人像だが、その「美人」ぶりはいずれの伝統とも隔絶している。

背景に藤棚が見え、庭で撮影されたことがわかるが、女と木は、庭ではなく、大地に直結し、深く根を張っているように感じられる。生命の樹と、胸をはだけて地をふみしめる地母神のイメージは、岸田劉生の《南瓜を持つ女》（1914, pl. 111）に通じるものがある。劉生には裸婦像は極端に少ないが、習作の他は聖母像に源を持った、優しい母性的な女たちである。（＊4）この《南瓜を持つ女》だけは、農婦を思わせる設定の、強い土俗性が異色である。

明治以来、洋画におけるヌードは、多くが西洋婦人をモデルとしてヨーロッパ的な美学に準拠するか、あるいは風俗画の伝統に拠ってきたため、力強い日本の裸婦が描かれることは、萬鐵五郎《裸体美人》（1912, fig. 1）までなかった。ゴーギャンのタヒチの女たちはよく知られておりその影響も指摘できるだろうが、《裸体美人》では、半裸の横たわった女が、性的ではなく功撃的で強靭な存在として描かれている点に、画期的な意識がかんじられる。写真においては、『明治裸体写真帖』（＊5）に見られるような痛々しいヌードはひそかに撮影されていたものの、それ自身のイメージや表現をそなえた作品となるには、やはり野島康三《樹による女》を待たねばならないだろう。これらの点で彼らは、同時代人として共通した美学を模索していたのかもしれない。

野島は、しばしば言われるように、どっしりとした肉厚のモデルを好んでおり、彼の中に健康な母性への憧れが底流していたことは否めない。しかし野島の裸婦に表現されているのは、全てを受け入れて慈しむ聖なる母性ではない。

不敵な《樹に寄る女》は、作者・野島にとって、攻撃的で異質な存在としてとらえられている。個体として生命を代表し、主張する女。野島の女性像の一貫した特徴が、すでにここによく表れている。野島は、女性に個性や人格を見るよりも、常に、生命体を代表するような神聖な官能を見ていた。

描き起こされ強調された両目で、はっしとこちらをにらみすえるこの女は、野島の前でカメラをまともに見返した最初の人物でもある。同1915年から1923年ごろに集中して制作された野島の肖像写真（主に男性像）は、《風邪の少年》（1920, pl. 13）を除いて皆、安定したポートレイト構図で、一様に目線をそらしている。表情と感情を一切押さえこんだ彼らは、求心的で謎めいた内面をそなえ、硬直した威厳を持つ深刻な人物像である。

野島は1910年代半ばの岸田劉生の肖像画を高く評価していたはずである。彼は岸田作の《川幡正光氏之像》（1918, pl. 110）を苦労して購入した。肖像画における岸田の理想主義的な画風は、明らかに野島に影響を与えている。長く変わらない野島の「写実は芸術の本道だと思ふ。」とする考え方は、岸田の影響のみならず、自然＝対象への畏敬に支えられていて、写真家として重要な考え方である。一方の岸田は、写真好きでことあるごとに写真館に行っていたのに、写実を極めるような自身の画業と写真の関係について、完全に無頓着であったのは奇妙なことといわざるをえない。ここでは詳しく述べられないが、そこに日本の近代絵画と写真の転倒した関係の一端がうかがえるであう。（＊6）

それはともかくとしても、《樹による女》の強く見返すまなざしの他者性は、野島の初期裸婦像のなかで異色であると同時に、彼が女性に見い出だそうとするものを代表している。生命感を主張する神話的でさえある存在は、当時の視覚芸術の先端と通底する、新しいイメージだったのである。

3———中間期（1920—1929）

1920年、野島は東京写真研究会展の第三室で個展を開く。この際、裸婦作品3点は警察の手によって撤去された。黒田清輝の裸体画事件から30年近くが経過していたが、当時もやはり裸婦写真が受け入れられる状況ではなかった。裸婦写真の発表は極めて少なく、モデルも不足しており、発表されてもほとんどが顔を隠したポーズであったという。野島も《樹に寄る女》のような野外の撮影は、その後長く試みていない。時代の条件が整わなかったためであろうか。翌1921年の裸婦作品は、人体デッサンのモデルとほぼ同様のポーズと構図である。人物は硬く、習作的な作品である。

4———1930—31年の裸婦連作

野島康三の裸婦作品がその頂点をなすのは、1931年の連作においてである。この年は野島にとって大きな分岐点だった。翌年からは新興写真への傾倒が明らかになり、後期の様式に移行する。後に述べるように、人物は風俗的、刹那的に描写され、断片化されていったのである。野島の1931年は、造型意識の高まりから、フォルムとヴォリュームの構成が研ぎ澄まされ、より明快になった年であると同時に、野島が育ててきた自然＝生命への畏敬が、観照によって彼の内なるエロティシズムと融けあった時でもあった。一種神秘的な、存在するからだの触覚が、「とろりとしたとけあった美しいふくらみのある面」（＊7）に実現されている。精緻なマチエールこそ、絵画に従属することのない、野島の表現としての写真を支えたものである。この多産な年は、ブロムオイルのデリケートな光の質感の微妙な深い調子が、ひとのからだの存在から受ける神秘的な官能と深いところで一致した、その極まりの時だったのである。

　一連の裸婦作品には、背景に屏風が使われた。これは光線を微妙

fig. 1：萬鐵五郎／裸体美人／1911

fig. 2：恩池孝四郎／浴後／1926

にコントロールする道具であると同時に、単純化した背景を、細い垂直線で強固に構成する働きをしている。ほぼ画面いっぱいに、裸婦は緊密な空間に密閉されて、ちょうど《仏手柑》(1930, pl. 28) がそうであったように、かえって無限定の時空間を獲得し、鋭敏な触覚を発酵させたような存在の密度をもつのである。

鏡や水盤をじっと覗く女たち (pls. 47, 56) は、自身の体感に沈みこみ、孤立している。野島の仏手柑や枇杷のように、厳しく世界に投げ出されていても、彼女たちは自分の内なる生命のために、充足しているようにみえる。母性的でも攻撃的でもなく、イデアルな生命の一個の現れとして、堂々とエロティシズムを引き受けているのだ。

そのなかでも、殊に質の高い表現は、顔を伏せた《題名不詳》の2点の裸婦像 (pls. 48, 50) に見ることができる。2点は、一方が求心的な静、他方が遠心的な動ともいえるほど、対照的な裸婦像である。他の同時期の作品は、ある瞬間的な表情やしぐさを強調する新興写真的な要素をすでに表しているが、2点のヌードは、要素をぎりぎりに切り詰めてあり、野島独特の存在の感覚が最も純化されている。

顔を伏せた裸婦は、細部を捨て抽象化されて、写真というメディアの即物的な性質を脱している。野島は、抽象的に有り始めた存在、最初の他者としての裸婦に、強くひきつけられたのではないだろうか。彼女たちは、充足した他者の、不思議なエロスを持っている。彼女たちはもはや母性的ではない。また、凝縮したフォルムを刻みつけられていても、未だオブジェとして扱われてもいない。その狭間の時期に、野島は全く独創的な裸婦像を撮ったのである。

彼のいう「與へられてゐる美をめがけて寫」すこと、「明暗、形の美によって對象を充分に生かした仕事」をするということは、この年の裸婦作品に最もあてはまるのではないだろうか。野島はその後手帳に〈小説と実話〉とタイトルをつけて、写すことと表現することについて「作品としては作者の意思、感情が織り込まれてゐなければそのものは生きてこない。そうでなければ説明的写真に過ぎない。」と書いている。彼の指す「小説」とは、リアルなものを見い出だす力のもとで、「実話」を生かせるような方法を創出することなのであろう。それがすぐれた〈見る人〉であった野島の、写真と表現の統合のしかただった。

こうした独自の裸婦像に到達するまでに、野島はおそらく梅原龍三郎の裸婦像にひかれてこれを研究している。座ってくつろいだり、鏡をのぞきこむポーズには、野島の写真作品への影響を指摘できるかもしれない。梅原を師に選んで絵画を学んだ野島は、彼の油彩画《裸婦》(1929, fig. 4) の作品に見られるように、赤と緑で厚く塗り込め、輪郭線で強く縁どった、力強い梅原の裸婦像を受け入れている。　梅原はルノワールに師事し官能にみちたやわらかな女性を描いていたが、帰国後には、多くの留学帰朝者と同じく、「日本の油絵」の創出という困難な課題に直面した。野島と知りあったのは、帰国の2年後ごろだったらしいから(*8)、二人の交友は、梅原様式が完成されてゆく期間と重なっている。梅原の裸婦は、常に

ほぼ全身像で、コラージュされたり分断されることのない、豊麗な官能と強靱な実体を持っていた。野島はそこにひかれたのであろう。梅原から譲られたマイヨールの座裸婦像を野島が愛蔵していたところにも、両者に共通する志向がうかがわれる。

梅原は桃山的な図案模様と日本女性のどっしりしたからだを組み合わせ、徹頭徹尾、「女」の肉体礼讃を繰り広げた。彼は自分の「日本の油絵」に、豊かな町人文化に通じる脈を掘り当てたのではないだろうか。一方、野島のこの時期の写真作品には、梅原の豪奢で装飾的な要素とは逆に、シンプルな形態の中に内面を求める、精神主義的な態度があらわれている。野島の裸婦が、どこか土俗的なふてぶてしさを持ちながら、常に純化された生命をかんじさせるのは、そのためかもしれない。

野島の1931年の裸婦は、同時代絵画を消化しそれに拮抗するブロムオイル・プリントの表現を修めて、モダニズムへと流れ込む寸前に、彼の持ち続けてきた「感覚の美」を近代的な造型感覚で洗練し、自然の存在＝生命への深い敬意を結晶化しえた、稀生の表現だったのである。

5───野島とモダニズム

《裸胸婦》の構図は、恩地孝四郎の《浴後》(1926, fig. 2) と似通っている。恩地は1920年に兜屋畫堂で初個展を開催したこと以外、野島との交流についてはわかっていないが、恩地自身『飛行官能』(1934) という写真を含む詩画集を出版するほど、写真には興味をもっていた。恩地にとっての写真は、もちろん新興写真である。恩地は独特のやり方で、野島よりよほど本質的にモダニズムを受け入れていた。抽象作品も多く手がけ、表現主義、キュビスム、未来派などの影響を顕著に受けた恩地は、モチーフの人物を、一個の全体としてよりは分割可能なフォルムとして扱った。恩地の裸婦は、非常にしばしば幾何学的に分断され、切りとられた部分の反復として表れる(fig. 3)。こうした感覚は、あるいは新興写真から得たのかもしれない。

野島が《裸胸婦》ですでに持っていた、幾何学的なフォルム構成への関心は、1931年を境に、急激に高まった。まず《題名不詳》(1931, pls. 49, 53) のような部分像が盛んに制作されるようになる。フォルムとしては完成しない「足」の中途半端ななまなましさは、やがて、《静物》(c. 1940, pl. 95) のような、足をオブジェとみなすフェティッシュな作品へと変化してゆく。これらは、「自然の姿、生き生きとしたところをつかむことが重要である。」(*9)という、従来の自然主義的な野島の立場とは断絶した表現である。

この頃を境にして、野島は新興写真へとのめりこんだ。当時彼は、「芸術写真といふとぼやぼやしたものや不鮮明な、なんだか意味ありげなものや、変に深刻めいたもの、薄い弱々しい気分あり気なものであった。然し今はそんなものを要求してゐる時代ではない。」(*10)と手帳に書きつけている。野島はブロムオイル・プリントを捨て、シャープなゼラチンシルバー・プリントを選んで変貌してゆく。「弱々し

い甘美の世界」(*11)という自らの言葉で、野島は自分の今までの作品を否定しようとしたのだろうか。写真界にドイツの美学が受け入れられ、野島も、科学、機能、機械、技術といった単語で写真を語ろうとし始める。

そこに洋装・断髪の、享楽的な女たちが出現する。ハイヒールを履いた足を高々と組み、また煙草を吸い、あるいはボアをまとって、野島の女たちはからだの原初的な尊厳を隠してしまった。ストライプの絨毯やモダンなインテリアのなかで、彼女たちは無意味にほほえもうとする。刹那的な風俗、現象、そうした表面的なものに注がれる感覚が、主題となってくるのである。この変化は、なにものかの崩壊さえかんじさせる。野島は着物を洋服にあらため、パイプをくわえ、自宅で毎週ダンス・パーティーを開くようになった。生活・し好を変える決心をしたのである。

野島の変貌を、伊藤俊治氏は"都市の女たちの発見"として、日本の急激な近代化・都市化と対応させ、そこに「日本」の「歴史」の大きな裂け目を見い出している。(*12) 雑誌『光画』を発刊してからの野島は、「女の顔」という見事な連作を発表した。しかし彼の写真はこれを最後に急速に弱まり、独自の美を失ってしまうのである。先の手帳に、「日本人だから日本人らしいものを作らねばならぬといふきゅうくつな考へは不要と思ふ。」という言葉があった。野島は、一層「日本的」な油絵へと向かってゆく梅原や、南画を研究した萬、早い晩年に完元画に沈潜した岸田劉生をどう見ていたのだろうか。海外へはほとんど出かけたことのない野島の日本観についてはこれしか残された言葉はないが、画家たちとの深い交友が、この頃から徐々に疎遠になってきたのも隅然ではないだろう。野島の作品は空虚な実験を経て、質量ともに衰える。彼はここで本質的な転向をした。

彼の転向は、未だ解決されない問題をわたしたちに提示してはいないだろうか。(みつだ・ゆり／渋谷区立松濤美術館)

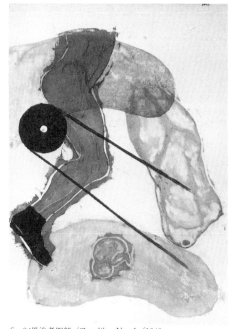

fig. 3：恩池孝四郎／アレゴリー No. 1／1948

fig. 4：野島康三／裸婦／1929

註:
（1）福原信三、淵上白陽、高山正隆、日高長太郎らが挙げられる
（2）別稿「〈見る人〉としての野島康三」参照
（3）「裸体表現の変容」宮下規久朗（三彩1990年10月〜11月）
（4）岸田劉生作「エターナルアイドル」(1914) に最もそれが顕著に表れている。
（5）「明治裸体写真帖」（有光書房、1970年）。ポルノグラフィー的な販売用写真や娼妓らを撮ったものが集められている。
（6）岸田劉生はおびただしい記念写真、ポートレイトを残している。アルバムには、岸田自ら撮影した写真も数点残されている。しかし、彼の芸術論には『写真』という言葉は出てこない。この点について、浅野徹氏に貴重なご示唆をいただいたことを感謝いたします。
（7）「野島氏の作品について」山崎静村（写真月報、1920年4月）中に引用されている野島康三の書簡のなかの言葉。
（8）「野島康三君の想い出」梅原龍三郎（野島康三遺作集、1965年）
（9）「人物作畫法」野島熈正（アルス写真大講座、1929年）
（10）野島康三の手帳より引用。手帳とあるのは、すべて同一のもの。年代は1932〜33年のものと思われる。
（11）同上から引用。
（12）「"都市の女たち"の発見」伊藤俊治（カメラ毎日、1983年6月号）

Introducing Yasuzo Nojima

Jeffrey Gilbert
independent curator

This essay began as a general introduction, but I must ask to be excused and allowed to digress for a moment. My research is hardly on a par with the scholarship or talent of many of the individuals I am about to introduce, and the accumulated information on the variety of subjects herein is a far cry from knowledge. My interest in the correlations and development of art and photography in Japan began in 1976. The following year, I was introduced to Nojima's photographs by Kanbei Hanaya a photographer born at the turn of the century whose career blossomed in the early 30's, and was deeply inspired by Nojima's efforts. Mr. Hanaya admired every aspect of Nojima's work, and everyone who met Mr. Hanaya was impressed by his selfless effort to share his enthusiasm. He worked to provide many opportunities for Japanese amateur and professional photographers to be seen and appreciated by a public audience. This exhibit had been Mr. Hanaya's dream for many years, but two months before the opening he passed away.

The following is an appreciation of Yasuzo Nojima, with hope that the presentation of his work will contribute to world understanding through the universal language of the arts.

Nojima was born at Urawa, on the outskirts of Tokyo, on February 12, 1989. His family had been well established in Tokyo for many generations and his father was an executive of the Nakai Bank, a major financial institution in the new industrial state. Records on hand show that by 1700 Nojima's family was employed in Edo as the licensed purveyors to Tokugawa Shogunate. Their financial success is born out by their long-standing relationship as major contributors to the Kotokuin Temple, the Temple of the Great Bhudda in Kamakura. Kotokuin is one of the principal temples of the Jodo sect of Bhuddism, and Yasuzu Nojima and his forebears are interned there. The family's material well-being and social security would be significant assets to his pursuit and support of the arts.

From 1905 to 1912 Nojima attended Keio University in Tokyo. Keio University was founded in 1867 by Yukichi Fukuzawa, a scholar and interpretor who became a leading social critic and theorist in the Meiji era of modernization, and remains today among the foremost private Universities for the liberal arts. Nojima's instructors were from the latest generation of Meiji Scholars to have closely examined Western systems of thought, and worked to integrate them in the context of Japanese social values. Many of them had studied abroad, and following their return began to replace foreign advisors and instructors who had been originally hired to facilitate the national programs of *bunmei kaika* [civilization and enlightenment] that characterize the last half of the nineteenth century. It is important to understand that central to the significance of what took place in the Meiji period is that, "Japan was not simply the passive object of "Westernization" after 1853 [when Commodore Perry first steamed into Uraga bay], but was to become an active participant in its own development as a modern society."[1] Japan was intensely engaged in a self-directed effort to actively import material cueture with an accompanying plural range of ideas, and access them through the processes of naturalization and/or symbiosis. Nojima

and his peers are often referred to as the first generation of Japanese university students to receive a thoroughly Western-oriented education that affirmed the power of self-endurance, a well developed self-identity, and adherence to a determindly humanist code of social behavior. During Nojima's student years, these new ideologies were advanced and contemporized through the arts.

Realism would become a cause célèbre for European art by the midst of nineteenth century industry and scientific thought, but stylistically it remained an unrecognized aspect of art in the Japanese mainstream. There was evidently no official office that included a specific department for the study of Western art until 1861, and even then it was only considered as one more form of potentially useful technology. In 1857, new foreign settlements opened at Yokohama and at Hakodate in Hokkaido, and Japanese artists had an increased opportunity to meet foreigners with varying degrees ot artistic skill. For instance, the painter Yuichi Takahashi (1828-1894) mentioned in Kohtaro Iizawa's essay visited Yokohama in 1863 in hopes of seeing the English correspondent and illustrator Charles Wirgman, and unexpectedly met Wirgmans's partner the photographer Felice Beato. Yuichi was a self-taught artist working in Western-style oils who became impassioned with his rediscovery of Kokan's writings, and dedicated himself to the "truth" Yuichi is particularly significant in the history of Japanese painting for being recognized as the first Japanese artist to perceive that "truth" could be more than simply the techniques of realistic depiction: For Yuichi, Truth was the essential element of art.

The practical invention of photography is formally recognized as occuring in 1839, with distinctly different processes announced by the painter Louis Jacques Mandé Daguerre in France, and the scientist William Henry Fox Talbot in England. The inventors had been motivated by multiple causes and adjacent developments necessary to support the start of the photographic era. Among these were; the fledgling industries and workshops for chemical and mechanical supplies, a long and diverse history of experimental inquiry leading to the initial popular acceptance of scientific method, and established modes for the representation of truth in pictorial strategies that included the first trends towards the aestheties of nineteenth-century contemporary Realism. The first currently known camera set arrived in Japan in 1848, and merged with these essential modern elements that had all come through the minuscule access to the Western world maintained at the port of Nagasaki. This knowledge and new technologies served as precursors in Japan to the establishment of modern industry, and scientific practice. The new perception of the world based on material logic dedicated to the 'representation of truth' was initially written in Japanese as *shashin* (literally, "copy truth"). This term remains operable today as the Japanese linguistic sign for 'photography.'

The Realist novel and Naturalist movements were forged at the start of modern Japanese literature by authors and critics who placed particular emphasis on observable phenomena, and attended to actuality perceived through the senses. Their work, published in daily installments by the major newspapers, created an increasingly visual account of contemporary Japanese life. One of the most frequently read and influential figures from this period is Soseki Natsume (1867-1916).[2] The principal characters in his 1906 novella *The Three-Cornered World* [*Kusa Makura*] are a woman of strong independent character and a painter in the "modern style." Their ensuing dialogue serves for the author as artist to visualize Japan's entrance into the modern world. *Sanshiro* (1908) explores the title character, a young man from the provinces, coming of age at Tokyo University, encounters between urban intelligentsia, and first love. In the core of this novel, Soseki brilliantly sets out a very modern argument concerning media difference in the temporal and expressive limits of poetry versus painting based on Gotthold Ephraim Lessing's central proposition in *Laocoön : An Essay Upon the Limits of Painting and Poetry*. What I wish to emphasize is that something more than sophisticated literary appropriation was taking place. The new literature fervently discussed artistic production as a mode for expressing modern conscience, and invoked the discourse of individuation and alienation. The new wave of young artists and intellectuals were inspired to pursue the cause of individual self-expression, and became some of the chief protagonists of the modern scene. In this milieu Nojima seriously turned towards art, experimented with Western-style oil painting, and began to create his first photographs.

In 1907 Nojima submitted his work to the Tokyo Photographic Study Group (Tokyo Shashin Kenkyu Kai, 1907-present), at the start of this important organization for pictorial photography. Between 1904 and 1909 the society's first director Tetsusuke Akiyama (1888-1944) translated foreign publications and introduced many of the pigment processes favored by pictorial photographers throughout the West.[3] The Tokyo Photographic Study Group was supported in part by Konishiroku, one of the first Japanese manufacturers, importers and distributors of photographic supplies and materials. Increased ease of access, commercially produced materials, and improved availability suddenly brought photography in Japan within the range of an expanded group of individual practitioners. This was a significant change from the commercial photographic studios that had produced the vast majority of the photographs in the previous century. The rise of photography as a private pursuit brought amateurs into the field who envisioned picture making as an aesthetic pastime, it also found a few individuals who were prepared to pursue photography as an art.

Nojima received praise and recognition for the early accomplishments he submitted to the annual exhibitions at the Tokyo Photographic Study Group, which was the major salon for pictorial photography in Japan. This activity closely parallels the developments in the Photo Club de Paris, the Linked Ring in England, and the Photo-Secession in the United States. By 1911 the salon had advanced to a level where Seiki Kuroda served as a juror.[4] *Muddy Sea*, 1910 is the earliest photograph in this exhibit, and seems to draw its model from both the content and goal of the academic mainstream in Japan of painters working in the plein-air manner. It also in part stands on the cusp of the shift from realism to more subject oriented art. In the midst of his first efforts to master the craft and come to terms with the tradition of photography, Nojima discovered that his new found chosen media for expression could be driven and sustained by his development as an artist. This critical sense of awakening was a formative experience that Nojima shared in common with other artists emerging in this period. Bonds formed in the cause of self-expression were supported by the growth of ideas affected by the long range developments that had been taking place in Japanese culture and ideology.

It should be noted in regards to the sweeping changes that characterize the Meiji period, "It was not simple cultural mimesis or pure intellectual curiosity that led to the incorporation of Western ideas, but a strongly felt need for intellectual order in a context of grave psychological uncertainty."[5] In Nojima's university years, Western ideas continued to play a critical role as new alternatives to the uncertainties of referring to the disrupted history of the past, or accepting the instrumentalist polities of thought being handed down by what was amounting to a militant oligarchy fighting the Russo-Japanese War in 1904-1905, and annexing Korea in 1910. As new media and new ideas came into the twentieth century, and Japan completed the transition to an urban indurtrial economy, Nojima's generation were struggling to establish an identity for themselves as individuals in an international context. By the start of the Taisho period, the incessant vitality of first phase modernization entered a period of slackening. Amidst growing conservatism, many people began to internalize the question of loyalty and Japan's future in the modern world. They reacted by demonstrating the personal courage to protest the increasingly powerful, establishment bureaucracy by placing their livelihood and talent at risk in support of their idealism and search for individual truth.

Modern art entered the Taisho period with a series of radical departures from the juror's demands for conformity in the Western painting section of the official *Bunten* exhibit sponsored by the Ministry of Education (1907-present day Niten). A new generation of artists were striking out on their own to create independent exhibits and promotional strategies through informal associations such as the Fusain Kai (Charccoal Sketch Society, 1912-1913), Nika kai (Second Division Society, 1914-presest), Sodosha (Grass and Earth Society, 1915-1921), and Sosaku Hanga Kyokai (Creative Print Society, 1918). These artists demonstrated a passionate eclecticism and experimental search for personal style ranging from ; post-impressiosism, expressionism, fauvism, and high realism, to cubism and the start of non-objective art. Ryusei Kishida (1891-1929), Ryuzaburo Umehara (1888-1986), Tetsugoro Yorozu (1885-1927) and Kazumasa Nakagawa (1893-1989), painters and friends of Nojima's that are included in this exhibition, were the founders and principal members of several of these organizations.

The center for much of their activity centered in the Kanda section of Tokyo. It was much then as it is today, a part of the old city that includes publishing houses and both the new and used book districts. It remains a favorite haunt for writers, with a mood, perhaps, that would have also proved attractive to their contemporaries in New York. Directly after his return from Europe in 1910, the sculptor and critic Kotaro Takamura (1883-1923) started a gallery named Rokando in the Awaji Cho neighborhood of Kanda. Kishida Ryusei, who originally studied with Kuroda before striking out on his own, had a solo exhibit there in April of 1912. The *Yoninkai* [The Group of Four] Yasuzo Nojima, Ryotaro Ono, Seison Yamazaki, and Yoshio Yamamoto may have exhibited together at Rokando following Ono's one man show there during this period. Umehara studied in Paris from 1908-1913 where he was able to spend time with Renoir. Immediately following his return to Japan, he showed at the Venus Club in the Misaki Cho neighborhood of Kanda from October 5-14, 1913. Kishida exhibited there from October 16-22. Kishida had another exhibit at Mikasa a gallery in the Owari Cho neighborhood of the Ginza district adjacent to Kanda in March 1914.[6]

I have not been able to find much information regarding Nojima's activites in this period. In 1909 his work was included in the second juried exhibition sponsored by the Tokyo Photography Study Group, and he entered the College of Economics at Keio University, in preparation apparently to pursue a career in business. In 1910 he was included in the first annual members exhibit of the Tokyo Photography Study Group, and in 1911 left Keio University due to poor health. At some point in this period, Nojima received his family's support to pursue a career in photography and the arts. There are only a few pieces from this time, but already they demonstrate the combination of facile technique and serious intent that are characteristic of the work he created throughout his career. In 1915, he opened the Mikasa Shashin Ten (Mikasa Photography Place) in the Ningyo Cho neighborhood of Kanda. Nojima maintained his personal studio there, painted in order to better understand the nature of painting, and collaborrated with his assistants in the commission of fashionable photographic portraits. In the same year he also became a member of a Noh recitation group (*utaikai*) founded by the Realist poet Shiki Masaoka and joined by his close friend Soseki Natsume. The other members included a group of their disciples; Hekigoto Kawahigashi (poet), Kiyoshi Takahama (poet), Yoshishige Abe (philosopher and educator), Toyoichiro Nogami (Noh scholar and theater critic, husband of author Yaeko Nogami). The group studied with Shin Hosho, the herediary master of the Shimogakari Hosho Ryu School of Noh, and his assistant Kenzo Matsumoto. Their meetings frequently convened in Nojima's home. This group, particularly Nogami, contributed a great deal to the reevaluation of the litereture of Noh, and initiated public performance in the Taisho period.

Nojima's generation in the arts was largely dominated by the associates of *Shirakaba* (White Birch, 1910-1923), a journal devoted to new art. Theirs was an extreme sort of Naturalism, with a recurring message of individualism, and absolute artistic freedom. When *Shirakaba* started, many of the authors were still students at the Peers School (Gakushuin) in Tokyo. They studied, translated and published the writings of Western artists like Cézanne and Matisse, and began to introduce an eclectic history of art that ranged from Van Gogh, Rodin and the contemporary scene in Tokyo at one end, to the Quattrocento. This increased their following, as the practice of Art History was still in its infancy and the immediate developments affecting contemporary art had yet to be surveyed. *Shirakaba* sponsored a number of exhibits and published numerous reviews. Their literary experiments produced a new form the group is frequently identified with that was ostensibly autobiographical, and stylistically brilliant, but their idealism often lacked the ability to transcend a self-concern for particulars and become universal. *Shirakaba* set the tone for the romantic image of the artist seeking to discover and express their individuality in the Taisho period, but I believe it was the rigor, and keen focus on actuality of the modern realists that informed Nojima with the integrity of personal truth.

As his own work developed, Nojima was able to extended the his range of experience and ability to interact with his contemporaries. For one year, beginning in June of 1919, he opened Kabutoya Gado, close by the main intersection of Jimbo cho in Kanda. Kabutoya Gado was a gallery and gathering place that provided a regular venue for seeing works by contemporary Japanese artists that include members of the Fusainkai, Nikakai, Nihon Sosaku Hanga Kyokai, Sodosha and other associations. Perhaps the most significant accomplishment was simply that Kabutoya Gado served to bring this diverse body of artists under the same roof, and enabled them to show their respect for one another in a public setting. Kabutoya Gado was not a commercial venture, it was an experiment and a training ground. Nojima was constantly present, collected, made huge progress in developing his "eye for art," and formed many important friendships. If it was successful, I would like to think that Kabutoya Gado was a small, but significant annex for the experience of looking at exhibits of Japanese modern art being seen and integrated in the conscience of the Japanese public.

Following the close of Kabutoya Gado, Nojima continued to sponsor a salon open to the public in his spacious home. This was the site of critically important solo exhibitions for the gifted ceramic artist Kenkichi Tomimoto, and painters Ryusei Kishida, Tetsugoro Yorozu, and Ryuzaburo Umehama. Numerous reviews, and a large number of personal letters from the artists he exhibited, attest to his commitment. Many of the pieces exhibited can, in retrospect, be said to form the cornerstones of modern Japanese art. Nojima also helped to form the major modern art organizations of the twenties as a founding member of the Shunyokai (1922-present) which consolidated the members of Fusain Kai, Sodosha and Nika Kai, and the Western-style painting division of the Kokuga Sosaku Kyokai (1925-1926) which became Kokugakai (1928-present) where he joined Umehara as a founding board member. Nojima exhibited his own painting in each of these association's annual exhibitions.

Shirakaba, Chuo Bijutsu and other publications paid close attention to the artists shown by Nojima. In the accompanying articles in this catalog Yuri Mitsuda has carefully documented published records of the Kabutoya Gado exhibits.

This is the first time that Kabutoya Gado has been so closely examined in the context of an exhibition of Nojima's photographs, and it should prove to be valuable in many ways. Mainstream histories of Japanese modern art have overlooked, Nojima and this should emphasize our constant need to recorrect and recreate the historical memory. I have not been able to discover if any photographs were exhibited at Kabutoya Gado, but speculate that they were not. The easy suggestion is that in 1920 it was simply too early. There was no market for individual art photograpphs, and no professional career opportunities for art photographers. The economics of their position did not allow them the dignity to identify their particular pursuit of art as a bonafide career, their venues were constrained to amateur enterprise. However, "Amateurism seeks the development of the total awareness of the individual and the critical groundrules of society."[7] In this instance Nojima was an outsider, and seized the opportunity to work beyond the environment of official culture. I propose this in the sense of its being a liberating experience and proving ground for the development of his creative power. In 1920 Nojima had reached an initial stage of development that resulted in a small retrospective at the annual Tokyo Photography Study Group exhibit. The following comments are drawn from Seison Yamazaki's review of the exhibit.[8] From 1907, when he submitted his first photographs to the Tokyo Photography Study Group, until the opening of the Kabutoya Gado, Nojima's approach and philosophy of photography developed through three phases. The first was "unconscious," training his vision, trying to express meaning and find his own way, using the gum bichromate process to acquire more personal control of the final picture. The gum print was the popular choice for intentionally subjective works where it was desirable for handwork and control to be an obvious part of the composition. Through the practice of contemplation Nojima developed the intuitive understanding that things must be seen by ones own eyes, not by way of tradition or external beliefs. In this pursuit he was influenced by literary naturalism, and tried to work by observing nature and embodying the feelings he experienced in the picture.

Nojima's second developmental phase was "pictorialism." He increased his study of painting in order to extend his knowledge and practical experience of pictorial expression. He also explored many facets of Japanese traditional art. He worked deliberately, slowly, often taking months to produce the optimum print from one negative. Meanwhile he expanded his tecnique from gum bichromate, in which unwanted pigment is removed to develop the picture, and began to experiment with oil prints in which pigment is selectively applied. *Portrait of Mr. M.,* 1917 (pl. 18) is the only example we have of an oil print. The carefully balanced placement of tonalities and the use of the brush in the oil print also satisfied his painterly instinct. Nojima began to see the entire pictorial space as a unified whole, as opposed to previously attending to parts, which was a great leap forward. Working with the nude he began to deconstruct and simplify the face, rendering more detail in the body to concentrate the viewer's attention on overall form. At the start of his pictorial period,

Nojima opened the Mikasa Shashin Ten.

By 1919, when Nojima opened the Kabutoya Gado, his extensive study of pictorial expression and search for truth reached an impasse over the inherent contradiction of painterly photography and the final character of actuality in his work. He stopped working for several months, studied the visual art he exhibited at Kabutoya Gado and developed a, "platform for photograhic art" (*Shashin geijutsu no yobo*). Nojima began to concentrate on light, shade, and form, and the plastic quality of modeling light unique to the media of photography. It may also be said that one factor contributing to the power of his vision was due to his facile mastery of hand controlled techniques through which he achieved a transcendent quality of finish. As pointed out in Kohtaro Iizawa's article, his portraits from the 20s' are instilled with a powerful sense of existence.

Following the close of Kabutoya Gado in 1920, Nojima sold the Mikasa Shashin Ten and moved from Kanda to the Kudan district and opened the Nonomiya Shashinkan (Nonomiya Photo Studio). The name Nonomiya was taken from the title of a famous Noh play. The Nonomiya Shashinkan stood in a prime location northwest of the Tokyo imperial Palace. theKudan. Nonomiya was in business for over twenty years and became very well known for its portraits, and high level technical services. Following the Great Kanto Earthquarke of 1923, Nonomiya arose in the midst of the emerging new city on clean modern lines designed by the architect Tsuchiura Kijo, a student of Frank Lloyd Wright. The new Nonomiya building incorporated the studio on the ground floor of an apartment hotel, one of the first in Tokyo, built in the International Style. Nonomiya became an assembly point for many younger photographers in the start of the modern photography movement who sought out Nojima's advice and encouragement.

The inroads and dispersal of new ideas entering Japan are difficult to track with any certainty. Nojima left no memoirs or diaries recording the major influences he felt. The publications remaining in his library include virtually complete runs of the prewar issues of *Photographie* and *Das Deutsche Lichtbild*. He also supplied articles and was close to the critics and editors of the Japanese publications including *Arts, Asahi Camera,* and *Shashin Geppo* which attended to the Art Photography movement in the teens through the early-twenties, and later covered the Modern Photoghaphy movement from the late-twenties until the Start of the Pacific War. In 1931 the Asahi Newspaper Group sponsored the touring version of *Film und Foto,* the international exhibit organized by the Deutschen Werkbunds that carried the message of the New Photography around the world. The photographers Iwata Nakayama (1895-1949), and Kanbei Hanaya (1901-1991), both from Ashiya, organized the second exhibit (in Tokyo) of their Ashiya Camera Club (1930-1941) to coincide with this event and bring recognition to the avant-garde photographers emerging in Japan.

Exactly one year after the *Film und Foto* exhibit, Nojima realized the need for a new publication to carry the message of the modern photography movement in Japan, and supplied his personal funds to publish *Koga* (Light Pictures). From his base at Nonomiya, Nojima brought together *Koga's* principal members; the photographers Iwata Nakayama and Ihee Kimura (1901-1975), and critic Ina Nobuo. They were joined by Hara Hiromu, a typographer and graphic designer with close Bauhaus affiliations, who regularly contributed articles and layouts. *Koga* was published in eighteen issues from May 1932 through December 1933. During this period the members of *Koga* made a strong attempt to sustain and extend the new directions of photography, and publish the best new work being produced in Japan. Translations and editorials were regular features, and both national and international developments were examined by two of Japan's first professional, photography critics; Itagaki Takaho, and Ina Nobuo. Their coverage of the European avant-garde was wide ranged, and Ina's manifesto "Return to Photophaphy" in the opening pages of the first issue of *Koga* proclaimed the New Vision and Real Photo.

In 1933 Nojima and Hiromu Hara collaborated to produce a model photography exhibit *Works by Nojima Yasuzo, Photographs of Womens Faces, 20 Pieces*. The exhibit was held at the Kinokuniya Gallery, one of the major galleries at this time, in the Ginza district of Tokyo. Nojima and Hara wanted to create a novel installation plan that was as advanced as the photographs. Up until this time most photography exhibits had been treated like painting exhibits, or as large scale themed shows (travel, promotion, etc). They felt that approach created a negative conotation for their pursuit of a new art. Nojima produced twenty, 559×457 mm (22×18 inch) glossy enlargements of women's faces, and simply told Hara that he wished to exhibit them without glass, and wanted a title panel somewhere in the room announcing the exhibit. Hara created a design that specified the photographs be installed in even intervals on a white-painted, thin panel that ran around the room. These faces are a stark contrast to the skewed angle and radically cropped portraits, printed in bromoil, from the year before. The twice lifesize, unretouched headshots set in strong artificial light, set off against the white band on cool gray walls, produceed a dynamic effect. It appeared as if Nojima had carried his eye out into the psychological environment of the new city to create a pastiche of vogue fashon and glamor; recording the "new woman" in a startling collection of Real Photo's.

Other experiments followed, but it was becoming obvious by the time *Koga* ceased publication in 1933 that the modern photography movement was hard pressed to sustain itself. Fascism was abroad in the land, and both national and local authorities investigated the avant-garde for signs of anarchy or other subersive behavior. Nojima was able to open a photography division in Kokugakai in 1938, and exhibited a haunting set of photograms in their 1940 exhibit. In 1941, while many artists were enjoined to declare their patriotism by contributing to the offices of publicity and propaganda, Nojima responded to this pressure by publicly stating in the June issue of Asahi Camera Magazane, "Everybody has a right to choose to do art which satisfies himself. One cando news photography if this is what he wants to do, but I choose not to

do news photography." This was Nojima's spiritual farewell to many members of the modern and avant-garde movements.[9] Modern formalism or the hegemony of style were never a primary concern for Nojima, his eye for beauty plunged beneath the surface of things and he maintained a serene confidence in his sensitivity and self-awareness. Perhaps the finest example of this quality emerged in his 1930 still life *Bushukan* (literally: Bhudda Hand Fruit). In this work he achieved an internal harmony of purpose that went beyond the grasp of many other Japanese artists who had taken-up the forms of perception but were unable to come to terms with with their beliefs and accept their individual self-identity. This crisis sometimes led to extreme solutions: suicide for several authors from *Shirakaba*; the flight back-to tradition or domination of powerful, monadic art organizations by early independent Western-style painters. For others still, the exodus of the expatriate would supply an answer in the years ahead. Few remained from the original core of the modern movement to resolve the question of independence.

The prewar avant-garde and modern photography movement in Japan flourished as a vital experiment in the early-thirties until it was absorbed by the talent pool of advertising or the publishing venues of commercial photography. In the postwar era publication expanded, but Nojima's work was not appropriate to the milieu, his health declined and his domestic life was burdened with financial setbacks in the reconstruction period. He finally retired to the countryside outside of Kamakura. The individual artist, in seeking a place in contemporary Japanese society, continues today to be severely challenged. It is only in recent years that artists, historians, and other members of the art community, in the course of revising their understanding of the causes at work in their immediate past, have begun to discover Nojima's work and recognize the importance of his activities. For Nojima, who stood on the frontier of contemporaneity through three eras of change, the universalist's belief in the artist's purpose remained constant:

> The artist feels it is worth living as an artist when they can give joy and meaning to the public; they serve a great part as a human being. Even though the names or personal histories are unknown, the heart (*kokoro*) of the artist will dwell in the works and be alive. Anyone will do. I hope that everyone will produce fine work."[10]

NOTES
(1) John Whitney Hall, *JAPAN From Prehistory to Modern Times* (New York: Delacorte Press, 1970) p 243. This statement is preceded by, "Japan's confrontation with the West, like the earlier encounter with Chinese civilization, was to force a major turning point in its history. But the common assumption that Japan was simply overwhelmed by foreign influence holds no more for the nineteenth century than it did for the seventh ..."

(2) For English translations see: *The Three-Cornered World,* Translated by Alan Turney and Peter Owen. (Tokyo, Japan and Rutland, Vermont: Charles E. Tuttle Company, Inc., 1968). *Sanshiro*, Translated by Jay Rubin. (Seattle: University of Washington Press, 1977). Also: Donald Keene, *Dawn To The West* vol. 1 *Japanese Literature of the Modern Period : Fiction* vol. 2 *Japanese Literature of the Modern Period : Poetry, Drama and Criticism* (New York: Henry Holt and Co., 1984). To date, literature in translation, to a much greater degree than photographic reproductions of visual art, has been and remains the best introduction to the emerging psychological and social concerns of the individual artist and their identity in the establishment of Japanese modern art.

(3) Robert Demachy, a banker, popularized the gum print from 1895, and enjoyed an international reputation through the salon and publications of the fashionable Photo-Club de Paris. Among the other pigment processes Nojima used, the Ozobrome was invented in 1905 in England by Thomas Manley. The Bromoil process was developed in 1907 by the Englishman, C. Welborne Plper and E. J. Wall. Also see *The Complete History of Japanese Photography*. 12 vols., #2 "The Heritage of Art Photography in Japan", introductions in English by Jeffrey Gilbert. ed. by Dai Ichi Art Center (Tokyo : Shogakulan, 1985).

(4) Seiki Kuroda, "Tokyo Shashin Kenkyu Kai, Dai Nikai Ten" ["The Second Exhibition of The Tokyo Photographic Study Group"], *Shashin Geppo* (1911).

(5) Tetsuo Narita, *Japan : The Intellectual Foundations of Modern Japanese Politics*. Phoenixed. (Chicago and London : U. of Chicago Press, 1980) 86.

(6) According to an entry in Geibi magazine in May 1983, the gallery Mikasa ran from January 1914, to June 1915. The activities of these painters is discussed at length by Shuji Takashina, J. Thomas Rimer with Geraid D, Bolas, *Paris in Japan : The Japanese Encounter With European Painting*. additional entry by Donald F. McCallum. (Tokyo : The Japan Foundation, St. Louis : Washington University, 1987).

(7) Marshall MacLuhan and Quentin Fiore. *The Medium is the Message : An inventory of Effect*. (New York : Bantam Books, 1967). p93.

(8) Seison Yamazaki, "Nojima Yasuzo Shi no Sakuhin ni Suite," *Shashin Geppo* April (1920) : 246-253. Seison Yamazaki was a photographer and member of the *Yoninkai* [The Group of Four] with Nojima, Ryotaro Ono, and Yoshio Yamamoto.

(9) Important reference to this quote was made in Shigemori Koen's article, "Nojima Yasuzo, Unique Photography of the Nude," *Gendai Nihon Shashin Zenshu IV*. (Tokyo : Shueisha, 1978).

(10) Hiromasa Nojima, "Jinbutsu Sakugaho," in Ars Shashin Daikoza," *Ars Camera* (1927/1928) 1-14, (includes 5 reproductions of Nojima's photographs) This is one of the longest articles written by Nojima, and includes an extended series of statements regarding his views on making art. Nojima changed his first name to Hiromasa for a number of years in the Taisho period.

The basis for this essay was published in French as "Nojima et l'avant-garde," in the catalog *Japon des avant-gardes 1910-1970*. (Paris : Musée national d'art moderne, Centre Georges Pompidou, 1986).

I am indebted to The Nojima Collection, and its associates who have graciously responded to my questions for many years. The study of Yasuzo Nojima's career was helped in great part by Kohtaro Iizawa, his numerous essays and publications have become a standard reference. Numerous readers have patiently assisted in translating texts. The mistakes and misinterpretations are clearly my own. Lastly, I sincerely appreciate the support I have continuously received from my family.

野島康三　1910—1932
Yasuzo Nojima, Photography 1910—1932

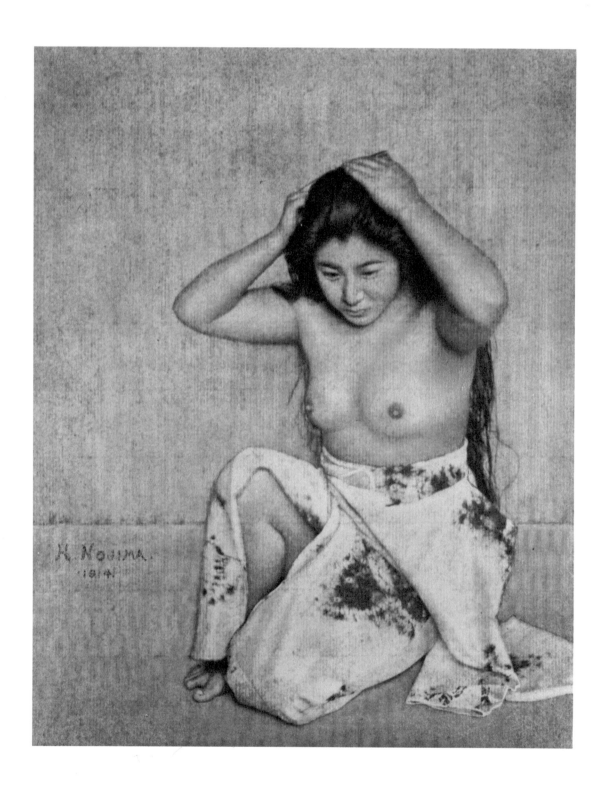

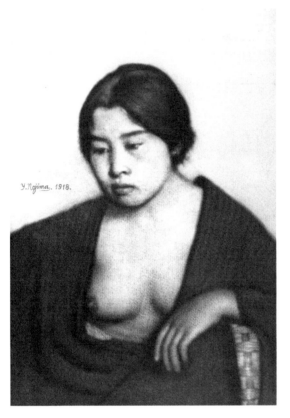

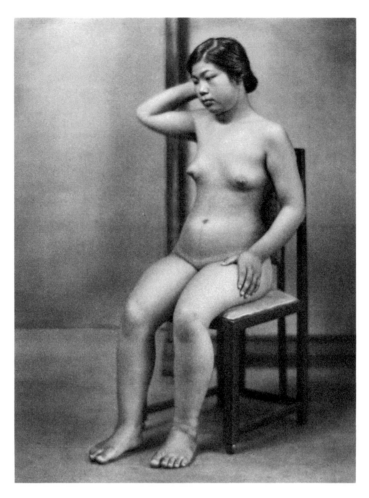

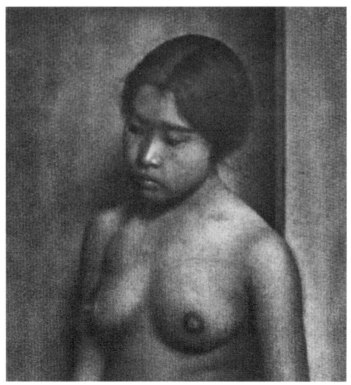

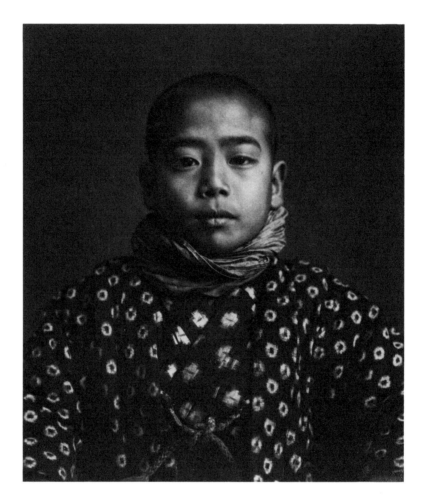

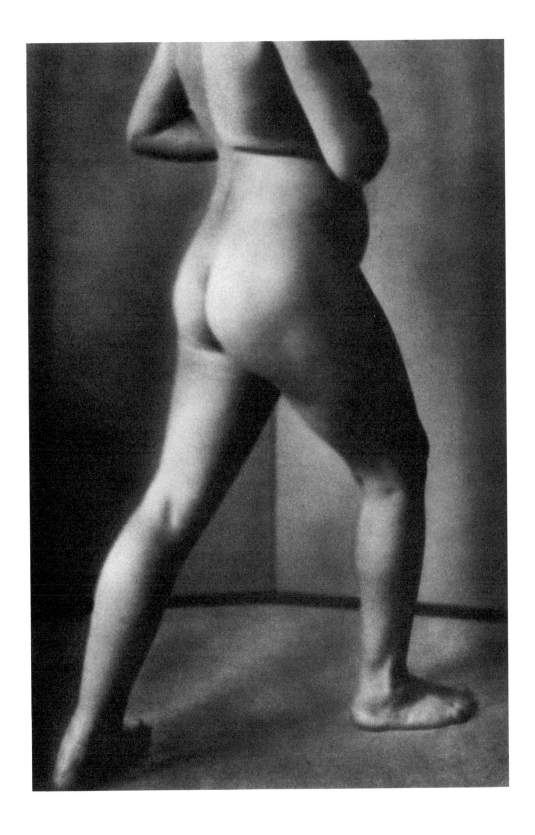

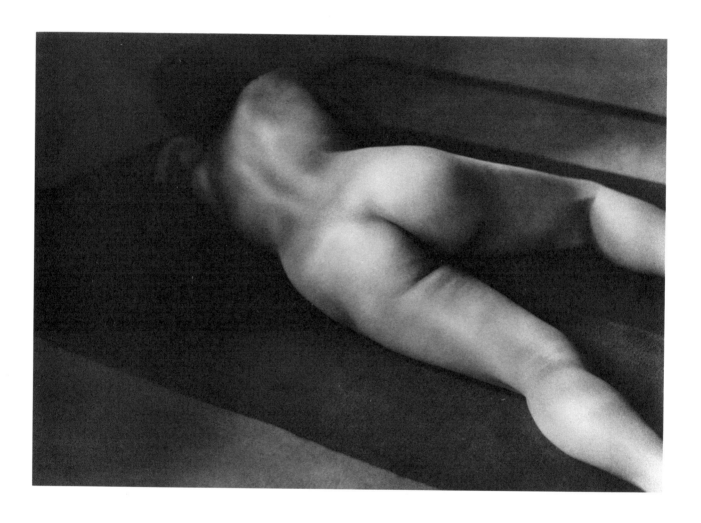

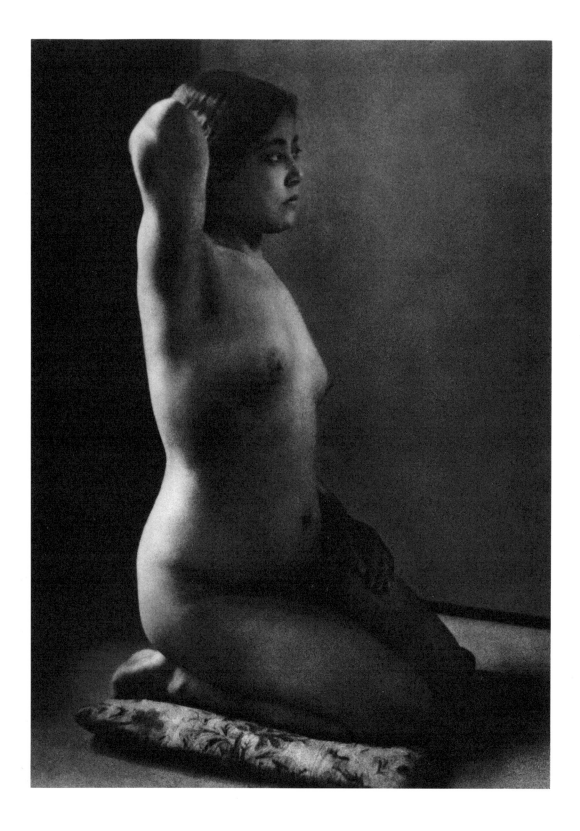

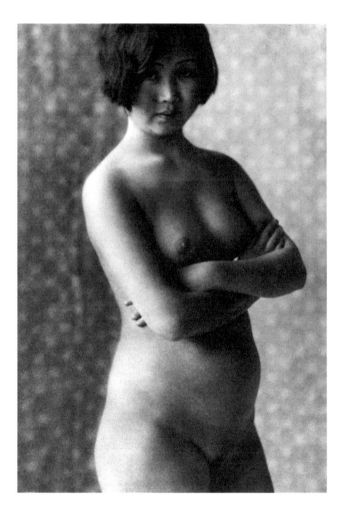

野島康三と同時代の画家たち
Nojima and Contemporary Painters

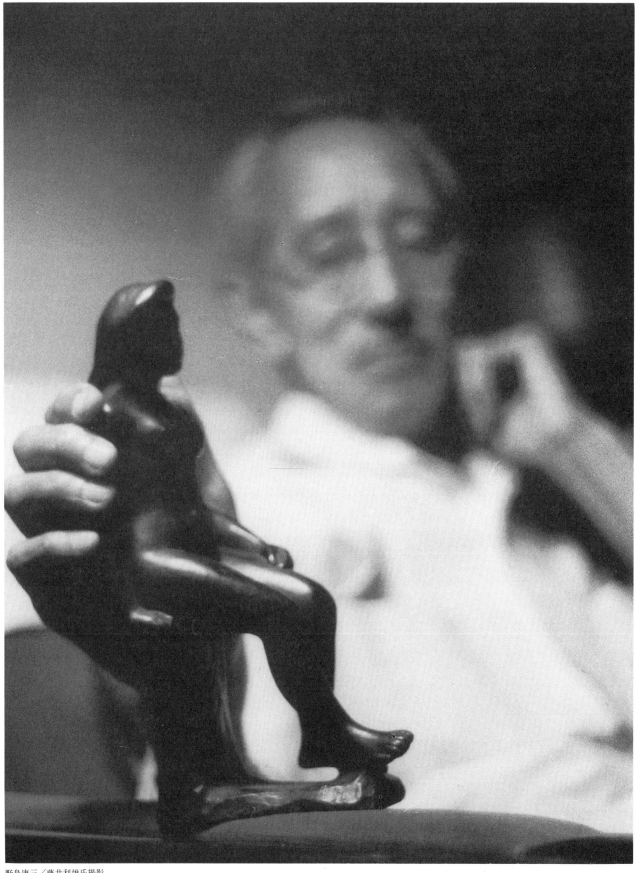

野島康三／藤井利雄氏撮影

〈見る人〉としての野島康三
展覧会企画と出版活動の記録

光田由里

野島康三のアルバムに、自分の屋敷やその庭先で、梅原龍三郎、岸田劉生、富本憲吉、萬鐵五郎ら様々な作家たちと並んで写った写真が何枚も残されている。痩せて背が高く、遠慮がちで穏やかな野島の表情は、どの写真でも変わることがない。

野島は、これら招かれた客人たちの、作品を購入し、定期的あるいは不定期の経済的な援助を与えていた。彼は旧幕御用商人の家筋に生まれ、日本の伝統文化に親しむ環境にあったが、銀行家となった父が新時代の教育を授けたため、新興ブルジョワジーの気風も身につけていた。野島が、当時の大家やアカデミックな権威ではなく、新進の作家や新しいジャンル―洋画や写真―に熱意を持って接したことは強調されていい。晩年、問われて自らを「美術愛好家」と名乗ったというが、彼は私的な意味でのいわゆる〝趣味人〟ではなかった。少なくとも、1920年前後から10余年間の野島は、画廊を開き、自宅を解放して作品発表の機会を提供し、出版に携わるなど、公的な活動にのめりこんでいた。「芸術＝美の魅力なくして吾人の生活が如何に無味乾燥なものであるか」と手帳に書きつけていた野島は、彼にとっての〈美〉について、ある種社会的な位置付けを考えていたようである。

彼はその活動の初期から、東京写真研究会の審査改革について発言し、「絶対に作家の芸術と自由を尊重していかなる作品も出陳せしめたい」と無審査の部を創設したり(＊1)、写真団体の会誌に、「真面目に本気になって」制作するよう呼びかける哲蒙的な作品批評を発表したりしていた。続いて、野々宮会という後進の勉強会を作ったことも、『光画』を出版し、読者との自由な意見交換を求めたことも、野島の一貫した意思の表れである。そこには確かに白樺派の作家たちとの交友から得た精神主義的な意識もあるが、さらにかんじられるのは、芸術の力を個人的な趣味の領域から解き放ち、社会の重要な要素としてともに高めてゆこうとする芸術観である。野島康三の写真は〈耽美的〉と評されることも多かったが、アマチュア写真界という閉じたサークルの中で、彼ほど表現を広い視野でとらえ、その果たすべき役割を考えた人物はいないだろう。

たとえ彼が病身や経済的状況の変化のために、この動機を短期間(＊2)しか表現できなかったとしても、その成果を見過ごしてはならないのである。

野島の同時代美術に対する視点をいま一度再構成してみれば、彼がいかに深い理解と先進性に満ち、重要な触媒的役割を果たしたかが、はっきりとわかる。

その活動を、現在確認される範囲で別表(p. 158-159)にまとめた。以下はその補足である。

大正 8 年(1919) 5 月、野島は神田裏神保町六に兜屋畫堂を開設する。商店街の並びの 2 階屋である。

彼は斎藤與里を相談役に、前もって周到な準備を進めており、開設に先立つ 3 月、上野精養軒で兜屋披露宴を催した。ここに招待されたジャンル、年齢、所属団体も様々な作家たちの助言や協力のもとに、野島は密度の濃い 1 年間の画廊経営に乗り出すのである。

開堂の５月３日、４日両日は招待日で、披露宴に出席した洋画家たちの絵画に、富本憲吉、中原悌二郎らの立体を加えた展示で幕を開けている。「美術愛好家の趣味が近時甚しく進取的になった。そう言ふ人の需めに応ずべく内質的眞價に重きを置き、不断の努力をする」旨の畫堂設立の趣意書も配ったらしい。(＊3)

当時は現在でいう意味の画廊自体がほとんどなく、京橋の田中屋、神田に琅玕堂などの先例があるものの、流逸荘くらいしかこれに比す画廊はない。美術雑誌に掲載された兜屋畫堂の広告(＊4)には、「洋画、日本画（洋画家）、彫塑、工芸品」と取扱いの範囲が示され、日本画は洋画家の描いたものしか扱わないという態度があきらかにされている。野島は売れ口の良いものばかりを扱う、当時の道具屋のような営業を拒否したのだろう。新思考の兜屋畫堂の活動は、ただちに注目を集めた。

所属団体を越えて若い有望作家を選んだ「新進洋画家新作展」、それまで公に展示されることの少なかったデッサンをとりあげた「兜屋畫堂第１回素描展覧会」、リベラルな審査を目的とした公募展「兜屋主催洋画展覧会」など、アイデアにあふれた企画は、当時大変斬新な試みであった。そのため多くの反響を呼び、美術雑誌『中央美術』、『みづゑ』、『現代之美術』などは競って兜屋の展覧会評を書き、読者からの感銘に満ちた投書も続々と掲載されたのである。「かかる意義ある展覧会を開いて呉れた兜屋畫堂主野島氏に深く謝す」という記事にもその反響はうかがえるであろう。

なかでも評価を得たのは、夭折の画家、関根正二と村山槐多のふたつの遺作展である。１、２階をすべて使い、代表作を網羅し、当時としては破格の、大部の展覧会カタログを製作している。関根展カタログに斎藤與里は、「何でも初めて君が兜屋に『子供』を出したとき、『俺の絵も兜屋に陳んだから是で死んでも好い』と云って嬉んで居られたそうです。」(＊5)とまで書いている。それはともかくとしても、この展覧会が開催されたために、二人のまだ若かった画家たちが人々の記憶にしっかりときざまれ、歴史に埋もれることを防ぎえた、とは言えないだろうか。

結成したばかりの装飾美術家協会の旗上げ展や白樺派の影響を残す「ロダン氏複製素描展覧会」、山本鼎の推す「児童自由画展」の開催後は、次第に若い作家の個展が主になってくる。時代順に近作をならべ、カタログをしばしば製作した。いづれの作家にとっても初めてないしは２回目の個展で、まとまって近作を展示できるまれな機会であった。これらの個展会場で、石井鶴三と中川一政が出会ったように、若い画家たちは知り合い、互いの影響関係を作っていったのである。切れ目なしの個人展覧会のなかでも、石井、中川、恩地孝四郎展は重要である。

野島はとりわけ中川、梅原龍三郎とは親しく交際した。彼が梅原の下で油彩画を学び始めたのもこの頃で、梅原の力に満ちた裸婦作品は、野島の写真に強い影響を与えることになる。また梅原にとっても、野島が毎年提供した熱海の別荘は、美しい光の、格好の写生場所となった。野島の別荘で、多くの梅原の代表作が制作されたのである。一方、中川に関しては、野島はすぐれたポートレイトを制作している。(pl. 19)また中川のスケッチに同行し、数枚のスナップ(fig. 8)も残した。これらは、中川の代表作《板橋風景》、《初夏水辺》(1919, pl. 143)の資料として貴重であろう。野島はしばしば、兜屋での展示風景や作品を撮影しており(＊6)、現存する一部の写真は、時代の重要な記録となっている。

こうしてジャンルや会派を超え、真摯に新しいものを選びとった野島は、各展覧会の出品作を毎回購入し、充実したコレクションを作り上げてゆく。このコレクションは野島邸に随時展示されていた。訪れた小林和作がこれに感銘を受け、中川、梅原に私叔することになる(1922年)など、逸話にはいとまがない。

そして１年後、突然以下のような閉堂のあいさつが配布された。

「……兜屋を開きましてから１年になりました。実に悦びに満ちた、幸福な１年でした。……別に理由があるわけではなく、只この仕事に飽きてきたのです。つまり私の我が儘です。兜屋は時期を得まして再興いたします。今よりももっとよいものになつて現はれることを信じます……。」

野島は経営の成り立たなかったであろう兜屋畫堂を閉じ、今まで経営していた三笠写真店を譲って、九段に野々宮写真館を開設する。

そして早くも翌年から、小石川の自邸で、サロンを解放した展覧会を開催した。

このとき開催した富本憲吉展は、以後の年中行事となった。野島は富本の作品を高く評価し、深い親交を結んでいる。この頃から富本が構想を暖めてきた「富本憲吉模様集」(＊7)は数年ごしに１巻づつ自家出版され、全３巻がそろったのは1927年である。この豪華な画集の製作に、野島は全面的な協力をし、克明な作品写真寄せている。192図版、筆跡も鮮やかに映えた見事な仕上がり（コロタイプ印刷）である。これを見た柳宗悦は、「画もさる事乍ら、写真に驚嘆す。写真家としての君の経歴の一エポックを劃すものと思ふ」と野島に書き送っている。(＊8)

中原悌二郎がこの年急逝し、没後出版が決まった彼の作品集のため、野島が作品写真の撮影を担当した。ここでも「ほとんど労働者の如く、終日立ち通しで、戸張君を相談役に、熱心に撮影せられ、尚現像の結果再三写し替へられたのもある。」(＊9)ほど打ち込んだ。『模様集』のシャープな撮り方とは異なり、照明でコントラストを強く出し、アングルを様々に変えて、複数の写真から作品の情感を複合的に伝えている。そこに野島の解釈がうかがえて興味深い。彼は中原作《憩へる女》を愛蔵していたが、1930年ごろ撮影された野島の裸婦作品に、それと通じ合う要素を指摘できる。(＊10)

大正11年(1922)は、野島の活発な展覧会企画活動の最後の年であった。翌年には関東大震災が起き、世の状況は大きく変化してゆく。いわゆるアヴァンギャルドの活躍が目立ち始め、文化を担う層も新しい〝大衆〟と呼ばれる人たちへと替わってゆくのである。

この年の野島邸での岸田劉生展は、麗子像のピークを成す作品で占められており、記念すべき展覧だった。岸田は以後、すでにこのとき示されていた東洋画への傾斜を強め、早すぎる晩年を迎え

てゆく。続いて萬鐵五郎は日本画展を開いた。言うまでもなく萬は、フォーヴィズム、キュビスムを解釈した、日本近代洋画屈指の偉才であるが、やはり晩年は南画・日本画の研究に至る。彼らは象徴的ではあるが特別なケースでは決してなく、留学帰りの洋画家の非常に多くも、後に日本的あるいは東洋的な画風に一斉に回帰していったのである。

かつて兜屋畫堂の経営方針に、「日本画(洋画家)」とわざわざ書き入れていた野島は、洋画と日本画の対立ないしは区分に対して、何らかの独自の考え方を持っていたのではないだろうか。野島が、浮世絵を参照した裸婦像から脱皮し、劉生のポートレイトや静物、梅原の裸婦をふまえながら独自の作風を作り上げ、のちにドイツ新興写真へのめりこんでいったことは、画家たちの日本回帰の動きと対照して考える必要があるだろう。(*11)

以上に概観した野島の交友関係は、残された書簡——いわゆる野島文書(別表参照)——からもうかがわれる。多くは連絡や挨拶、パトロンとしての野島への無心であるが、富本、中川のように自己の制作や心境について書き送ったものも多い。

野島文書は期間的に大変限られている。兜屋畫堂から『光画』までの時期に集中しているのだ。1940年代年以降は彼らと野島の交流はほとんど途絶えてしまった。戦後のどさくさで、モダンなアパートメントを併設した野々宮写真館を手放した後は、野島は病気のため葉山にこもることが多くなり、いつしかコレクションも散り散りになる。野島のエネルギーが公的な活動に使われていた時期が、彼の芸術家としての制作期間とほぼ完全に重なっていることを思うとき、野島の生きた時代の激しい動きとともに、彼にとっての〈美〉の意味がどのようなものだったかが察しられる。

見る人としての野島は、常にカメラを持っていた。彼は目撃し、見い出だした新鮮な〈美〉を記録し、擁護し、出版した。野島康三の写真作品は、こうした活動と合わせて立体的に見られなければならない。単に交友した作家たちの作風の影響を引き算してみるのではなく、穏やかな野島の、純粋な意図とするどい解釈を時代の中に読みとるべきなのである。(みつだ・ゆり/渋谷区立松濤美術館)

註:
(1)「展覧会に第一部第二部を設けるに就いて」野島康三(写真月報1915年4月号)
(2)野島の活発な活動期間は、1919—1923年頃および1930—1933年頃である。現在残されている写真作品からうかがえる範囲では、彼の実りある制作期間も、ほぼこれに完全に重なっている。
(3)〈覚帳の中から〉、中央美術、1919年6月号
(4)『みづゑ』、『現代之美術』、等の雑誌にほぼ毎号、展覧会の案内が掲載された。
(5)「関根正二氏遺作展覧会に際して」 斎藤與里(「信仰の悲しみ—関根正二遺作展覧会」、1919年、兜屋畫堂、所収)
(6)岸田劉生、萬鐵五郎、石井鶴三、富本憲吉からの書簡に、写真を送ってもらった礼状が含まれている。
(7)1924年—1927年にわたって、3分冊が発行された。富本自筆の序文に、「野島康三氏が写真撮影の多大なる労苦を重ね呉れられたると、伊藤助右エ門、柳宗悦両君が種々なる助力を与え呉れたるに対して記して感謝の意を表す。」とある。
(8)1926年6月1日付け野島宛て書簡より
(9)「中原君作品集の後に」 平櫛田中、『中原悌二郎作品集』1921年 日本美術院 所収
(10)中原悌二郎との関係においては、「中原悌二郎と野島康三」越前俊也(北海道立旭川美術館紀要 1989年 所収)がある。

fig.5:岸田劉生個人展覧会/野島邸/1922年5月25—29日

fig.6:梅原龍三郎氏画室にて/野島康三撮影/1926年1月

fig.7:萬鐵五郎日本画展/野島邸/1922年7月8—10日

fig.8:スケッチ中の中川一政/野島康三撮影/年代不詳

fig.9:富本憲吉氏作品展/野島邸/1922年12月21—23日

Yasuzo Nojima—A Clarity of Vision
A Record of His Exhibition Planning and Publishing Activities

Yuri Mitsuda
assistant curator, Shoto Museum of Art

In Yasuzo Nojima's family album, there are many photographs, taken at his mansion and in the garden, of him with such artists as Ryuzaburo Umehara, Ryusei Kishida, Kenkichi Tomimoto, and Tetsugoro Yorozu. The modest calm expression on the face of the tall slender Nojima remains constant in each image.

Nojima bought the works of the artists he invited to his house and provided them with financial support as well. While Nojima's birth into a family whose ancestors were shogunate merchants during the Edo period brought him into contact with traditional Japanese culture, his father, a banker, schooled him in the ways of the emerging bourgeoisie. What should be emphasized, however, was his passionate embrace not of the prominent or established artists of the time, but of young rising artists and new genres like *yoga* (Western painting) and photography. Though when asked about his profession in his later years he called himself "a lover of art," Nojima was no dilettante. Beginning in 1920, for more than ten years Nojima was publicly active in the art world—he founded a gallery, opened his estate for exhibitions, and published a host of art-related materials. For Nojima, who once wrote in his journal, "how dull our lives would be without the beauty of art," aesthetic beauty no doubt occupied a crucial postion in society.

As part of his early activities, Nojima—remarking that "we must, at all costs, respect the work and freedom of the artist, and do our best to exhibit whatever works they create"—helped the *Tokyo Shashin Kenkyu Kai* (Tokyo Photography Study Group) to reorganize their selection criteria and found a branch for the unjuried presentation of works.[1] In the literature of photography associations, his illuminating critiques of work called on artists to "approach their art with utmost seriousness." He also established a forum for younger artists —the *Nonomiya Kai* (Nonomiya Association), and published *Koga* (Light Pictures) magazine, in which he encouraged an ongoing dialogue with his readers —two more projects consistent with his ideas about Art. While it is clear that Nojima acquired some of his idealism through friendships with artists of the *Shirakaba Ha* (White Birch School), we also realize that Nojima believed both that art's power extended beyond the individual to affect society as a whole and that this power must be safeguarded. Though Nojima's photographs were considered "aesthetic," there were few people, if any, in the closed circles of amateur art photography groups whose vision was as broad as his or whose ambitions for the medium were as great.

Nojima's health was never good, and coupled with economic changes in the postwar reconstruction era, his major creative period was limited to the 20s' and 30s'.[2] His achievement, however, must not be overlooked.

By reexamining his approach to the art of his time, we gain a clear understanding of the depth of his knowledge, the foresight of his ideas, and his vital role as catalyst for the art of his time.

All that is presently known of Nojima's activities is listed in the chronology and the following will serve as a supplement to that chronicle.

In May 1919, Nojima established the *Kabutoya Gado,* a gallery in the Jimbo-cho section of Kanda in a two-story building on a shop-lined street.

With Yori Saito as his advisor, Nojima made careful preparations for the gallery, and in March held a reception at the Seiyoken in Ueno in advance of Kabutoya's opening. The guests at the reception represented all ages, genres, and art associations, and, thanks to their counsel and cooperation, Nojima embarked on a eventful year-long venture with the *Kabutoya Gado*.

On May 3 and 4—preview days for the gallery— works by the *yoga* painters who attended the Seiyoken reception, ceramics by Tomimoto Kenkichi and sculptures by Teijiro Nakahara were unveiled. "Recently, the interests of art enthusiasts have grown extremely progressive. In order to meet the demands of these people, we will endeavor to present artworks of substance." So read the gallery prospectus that was distributed at Kabutoya during this time.[3]

Then, only galleries such as Tanakaya in Kyobashi, Kanda's Rokando, and Ryuitsuso resembled those of today. The advertisement for Kabutoya that appeared in art magazines stated that the new gallery would handle *yoga, nihonga* (Japanese painting) by *yoga* painters, sculpture, and craftwork. That it would cater only to the *nihonga* of Western-style painters was indicative of the new gallery's stance regarding the Japanese artworld. Nojima no doubt rejected the practice —common among galleries then—of only handling marketable works and selling them like ornaments for interior decoration. His new breed of gallery soon attracted much attention.

Kabutoya held exhibitions brimming with fresh ideas and originality like *Recent Works of New Yoga*, which culled promising young artists from a variety of art associations: *Kabutoya Gado First Drawing Exhibition*, which afforded a view of *dessin* (a practice heretofore publicly ignored by the artworld); and public subscription projects with liberal entrance requirements like *Kabutoya's Yoga Exhibition*.

These shows won wide acclaim, and art magazines like *Chuo Bijutsu, Mizue*, and *Gendai no Bijutsu* competed with each other to review them. Their pages were also peppered with impassioned letters from readers impressed by Kabutoya's activities. The impact the gallery had on the viewers was expressed in a singular article by one writer who wrote, "I would like to offer my heartfelt thanks to Mr. Nojima of Kabutoya Gado for his fine exhibitions."

Two exhibitions of the posthumous works of painters Shoji Sekine and Kaita Murayama were especially well-received. In addition to filling both first and second-floor spaces with major works of Sekine and Murayama, Nojima also produced a substantial catalog (a rare commodity at the time) for each exhibition. In the catalog for the Sekine exhibition, Yori Saito remarked, "when Sekine first exhibited his painting entitled *Child* at Kabutoya he kept telling me, 'now that I have shown my work at Kabutoya, the Lord can come and take me away.'"[5] Though these two artists passed away when they were young, the Kabutoya exhibitions of their work made an indelible impression on the viewing public, and therefore ensured that their achievements would not be forgotten.

After holding such projects as the newly-formed Decorative Arts Association's inaugural exhibition : *Reproductions of Rodin's Watercolors* exhibition : and the *Children's Free Painting Show* recommended by Kanae Yamamoto, *Kabutoya Gado* devoted itself to one-person exhibitions of young artists. The gallery displayed these artists' recent works in the order they were made, and occasionally published catalogs. Since these exhibitions were usually the artists' first or second solo ventures, they afforded rare opportunities to see selected works of each artist. These shows also encouraged encounters like that between Tsuruzo Ishii and Kazumasa Nakagawa, and enabled young practitioners to come together and share ideas. Besides the exhibitions of Ishii and Nakagawa, that of Koshiro Onchi was also notable among this uninterrupted series of solo projects.

Nojima was particularly close to Nakagawa and to Ryuzaburo Umehara. It was during this time that Nojima began to study oil painting under Umehara, and the powerful presence of the painter's works of nudes becomes apparent in Nojima's photographs. Nojima's villa at Atami, which he made available to his friends every year, afforded Umehara the perfect lighting to practice his art. Indeed, Umehara painted many of his finest works at Atami. In Nakagawa's case, Nojima made an excellent photographic portrait of him (pl. 19) and also documented the painter on sketching trips (fig. 8). These latter photographs serve as vital documents for understanding Nakagawa's best works, *Itabashi Landscape* and *Early Summer Waterside* (1919). Nojima also actively photographed the installations and individual works shown at Kabutoya Gado,[6] and the images that remain serve as important records of the age.

Showing bias to neither genre nor group affiliation, Nojima only chose works he felt were sincere and new, and through his purchase of the art shown at each Kabutoya exhibition was able to amass a substantial collection, one which he exhibited from time to time at his residence. One anecdote among many has it that Wasaku Kobayashi visited the Nojima house, fell in love with the works of Umehara and Nakagawa, and became their disciples.

Then, one year after Kabutoya's birth, Nojima sent out the following news of its closing :

····Kabutoya has been open for one year. It has been a happy year of good fortune····When the time is right, Kabutoya will return. And I believe that it will reappear in an even more successful incarnation than it is now.

In 1920, Nojima closed *Kabutoya Gado*, transferred ownership of the Mikasa Photo Studio, and established the Nonomiya Photography Studio in Kudan.

And the following year, he organized important salon exhibitions at his Takehaya-cho residence. The Kenkichi Tomimoto exhibition held during this year later became an annual event. Nojima praised this artist's work highly, and the two men became close friends. During this time Tomimoto hatched an idea to present the designs for his ceramics in book form[7], and several years later self-published

the first of three volumes of *The Designs of Kenkichi Tomimoto*, the last being published in 1927. Painstakingly photographing the works for each volume, Nojima lent his wholehearted support to the production of these lavish catalogs. The books, printed in collotype, contained 192 illustrations which vividly captured Tomimoto's brushstrokes. Soetsu Yanagi offered Nojima the following praise : "The designs are beautiful, but the photographs are tremendous. They are major works in your career as a photographer."[8]

Teijiro Nakahara passed away suddenly in the same year, and Nojima was responsible for photographing his works for a memorial catalog in honor of the artist. Here again "Nojima worked like a laborer—standing all day long—and with assistance from Kogan Tobari set about photographing Nakahara's work, often reshooting work two or three times."[9] In contrast to the sharp focus found in the Tomimoto illustrations, here Nojima used his lighting to yield strong contrasts, and by taking one work from a variety of angles was able to present a composite sense of the work's content. Through these photographs we understand how Nojima interpreted Nakahara's works. Many of the elements in his photographs of nudes taken during the 1930s, betray Nojima's love for the sculptor's work *Woman in Repose*.[10]

1922 marked the end of Nojima's active role as exhibition planner. The Great Kanto Earthquake struck the following year and turned the world upside down. Out of the ashes avant-garde art movements and a new social class rose to shoulder the burden of culture.

1922 was also crucial in that it marked the full flowering of Ryusei Kishida's portraits of his daughter Reiko, an exhibition of which was held at the Nojima residence. After this time, Kishida's descent into the realm of oriental painting, quickened bringing about the premature decline of his painting career. Then Tetsugoro Yorozu followed suit by holding a show of his *nihonga*. Though Yorozu had achieved prominence in modern Japanese oil painting for his interpretations of Fauvism and Cubism, in his later years he became a devotee of *nihonga* and the southern school of Chinese painting. The reversion of these two painters was symbolic but by no means unusual—most of the artists who studied Western painting abroad returned to Japan only to lapse all at once into an embrace of oriental and *nihonga* styles.

Nojima had earlier expressed his independent stance on the issue of *yoga* vs. *nihonga*, when he specifically stated (in his prospectus for Kabutoya) that he would only accept *nihonga* by *yoga* painters. Shunning *Ukiyoe*-inspired nudes, Nojima, influenced by Umehara's nudes and Kishida's portraiture and still-life works, wrought his own style, and his plunge into works based on new German photography must be viewed vis-a-vis the regression of Japanese painters of the same era.

If we turn to the correspondence Nojima received from artists, the relationships outlined above can be explored in greater detail. While many of these letters take the form of greetings, or requesting Nojima's patronage, we can learn of their mental life and attitudes toward their own work through letters of Tomimoto and Nakagawa.

This correspondence flowered during an extremely brief

period between the time he opened Kabutoya until his founding of the magazine *Koga*.   After 1940, he had virtually ceased writing to his artist friends.   In the confusion of wartime, he had to give up the "modern" apartment building which housed the Nonomiya Photography Studio, sickness forced him to spend many of his days sheltered in Hayama, and his collecting activities gradually dwindled.   In evaluating his notions of *beauty*, we must remember both the tumult of his times and that his work as an artist overlapped the time of his energetic public activities in the art world.

For Nojima, seeing was everything, and he was never without his camera.   He recorded, protected, and published the *beauty* that he witnessed and discovered in the world around him. His photographs must be seen as solid proof of these vital activities.   His photographs cannot be reduced to merely an art determined by the work of his friends; the pure intent and sharp focus of the art of this mild man must instead be read in the context his age.   (translated by Charles Worthen)

Notes:
(1)   Yasuzo Nojima, "On Establishing a Two-Part Exhibition," *Shashin Geppo* (April, 1915).
(2)   Nojima was most active in the art world between 1919-1923, and 1930 -1933.   Judging from the dates of his existing photographs, these two periods overlap those in which he was most creatively fertile.
(3)   "From the Notebooks," *Chuo Bijutsu* (June, 1919).
(4)   Exhibition announcements were published in every monthly issue of magazines like *Mizue, Gendai no Bijutsu*.
(5)   Yori Saito, "On the Memorial Exhibition for Shoji Sekine," (*The Sorrow of Faith——the Memorial Exhibition for Shoji Sekine*, pub. by Kabutoya Gallery, 1919).
(6)   This includes letters from Ryusei Kishida, Tetsugoro Yorozu, Tsuruzo Ishii, and Tomimoto Kenkichi thanking Nojima for sending photographs.
(7)   This was published between 1924-1927 as three separate volumes.   In his foreword Tomimoto wrote: "I would like to express my deep gratitude to Yasuzo Nojima for his great labors in photographing my works, and to Sukezaemon Ito and Soetsu Yanagi for their kind counsel."
(8)   From a letter to Nojima dated June 1, 1926.
(9)   Denchu Hiragushi, "Afterword: The Works of Nakahara," (*The Works of Teijiro Nakahara*), pub. by Nihon Bijutsu In.
(10)   The relationship between Teijiro Nakahara and Nojima is furthered discussed in Toshiya Echizen's *Teijiro Nakahara & Yasuzo Nojima*, pub. by The Hokkaido Prefectural Museum of Art in Asahikawa (1989).

野島康三　Yasuzo Nojima

105：題名不詳（風景）／Title Unknown (Landscape)／1926
106：びわ／Loquats／1926

107：題名不詳（裸婦Ⅰ）／Title Unknown (Nude Ⅰ)／n. d.
108：題名不詳（裸婦Ⅱ）／Title Unknown (Nude Ⅱ)／n. d.

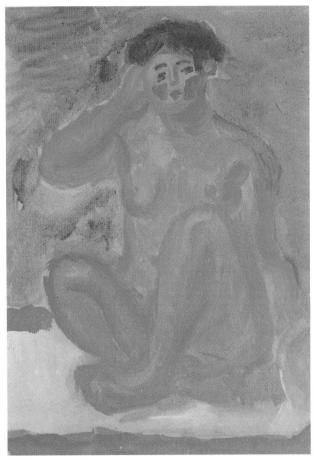

岸田劉生　Ryusei Kishida

109：裸婦（トルソー）／Nude (Torso)／1913
110：川幡正光氏之肖像／Portrait of Masamitsu Kawabata／1918

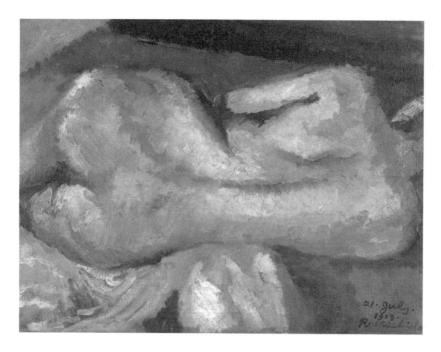

岸田劉生　Ryusei Kishida

113：村娘之図／Portrait of a Village Girl／1919
114：童児肖像／Portrait of a Little Boy／1921

岸田劉生　Ryusei Kishida

梅原龍三郎　Ryuzaburo Umehara

120：坐裸婦／Seated Nude／1918

萬鐵五郎　Tetsugoro Yorozu

萬鐵五郎　Tetsugoro Yorozu

136：湘南風景／Landscape of Shonan／1926
133：雪の景／Snow Landscape／1915

野島康三　1931—1951
Yasuzo Nojima, Photography 1931—1951

62：肖像（モデル F）／Portrait（Model F.）／1931
63：題名不詳（モデル F）／Title Unknown（Model F.）／1931

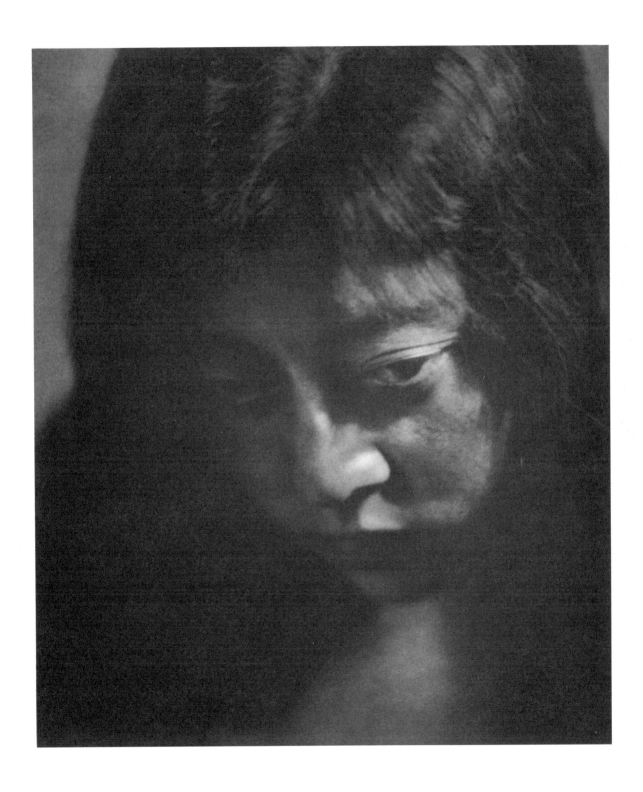

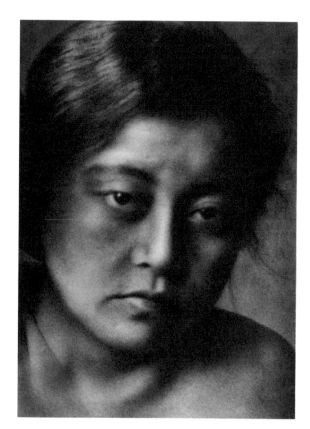 

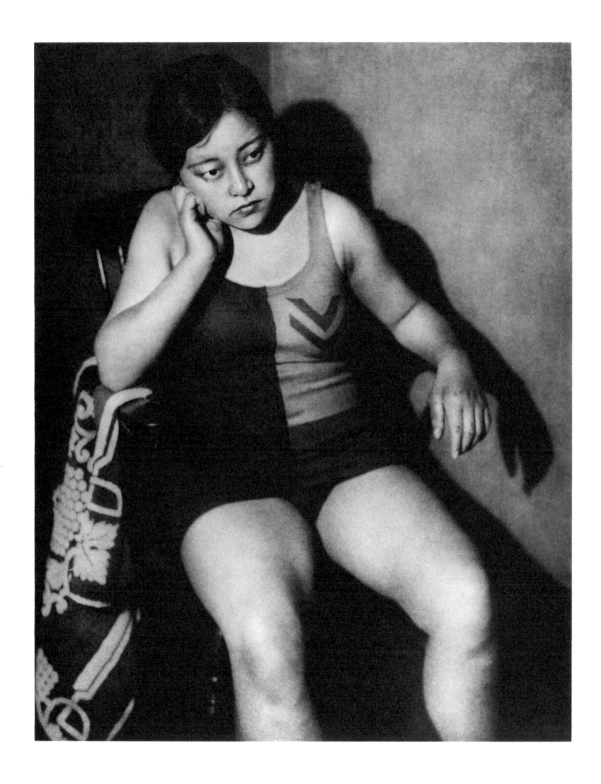

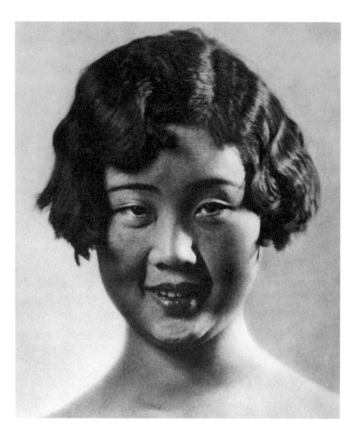

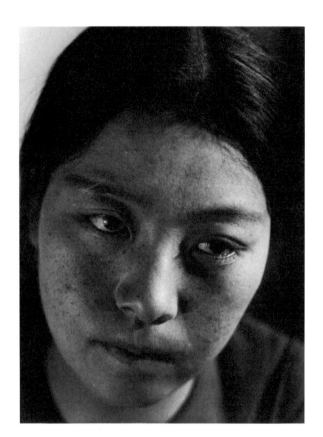

 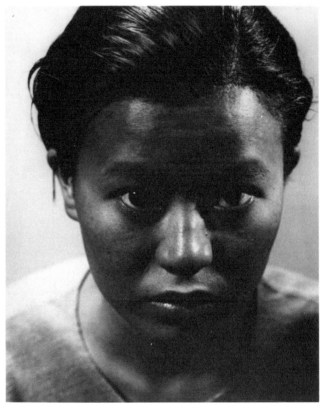

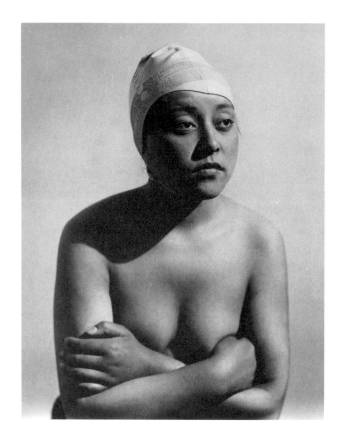

The Portraits of Yasuzo Nojima

Kohtaro Iizawa
Photography Critic

I think it was about twenty years ago when I first saw Yasuzo Nojima's photographs. The impression they made still burns bright in my mind.

They weren't original prints but images reproduced in *Nihon Shashinshi 1840-1945* (The History of Japanese Photography 1840-1945) (Heibonsha 1971). In the section "Art Photographs" were *Woman Leaning on a Tree* (1915, pl. 5) and *Loquats* (1930, pl. 32); and in "A Period of Discovery" were *Miss Chikako Hosokawa* and *Mr. Koreya Senda* (both from 1932, pl. 75, 76) and a series of photographs of nudes (1931-33) which began with images of "Model F".

Nojima's works struck me as possessing unparalleled strength; next to his photographs, the works of his peers pale. I cannot forget the steadiness with which his women stand upon the earth, or the surety of their gazes into the lens. While this book also initiated me to the sharp sense of the real in Nakaji Yasui's works, and the rich fantasy in the photos of Iwata Nakayama, it was Nojima's name that has stayed with me.

Not long after encountering this book, works of his on temporary loan to The Art Institute of Chicago returned to Japan and I had the chance to see them in the flesh at several exhibitions. Apparent here was a raw power that could not be savored in the reproductions. Beginning with "Taisho no Shitsukan" (*Taisho Jokanshi*) ("The Textures of the Taisho Era"—An Emotional History of the Taisho Era) (Nihon Shoseki, 1979), I have written various texts in an effort to draw closer to the secret behind Nojima's power. I have, however, only scratched the surface. Through viewing more exhibitions of his work and more writing, I will continue—with a blend of awe and homage—to chase Nojima's spirit.

There is no denying that the essence of Nojima's art lies condensed within his portrait photographs. Though his exquisite still-life photographs may embody the "love for things" of which Ryusei Kishida spoke in *Shajitsuron* (On Realism, 1920) and his sensitive landscape images of places like Karuizawa are unforgettable, the depth of his expressive powers is unmistakably greater in the more numerous portraits.

Moreover, the portraits occupy a crucial niche in the history of modern Japanese photography. Japanese photographers first began to use the medium as a means for expression in the latter part of the Meiji era (around 1900) after the promulgation of the notion of "art photograph." Led by the members of the *Yufutsuzu Association* and the *Naniwa photography Club* (both established in 1904)—who in their quest for the *art photograph* proclaimed "the image itself as the solitary goal" (Murasaki, *Utsusemi # 1,* 1904) —amateur photographers competed with each other to develop different techniques.

At the time, most of the ire of these amateurs was reserved for the portrait photograph—thought solely to be the province of the commercial-studio photographer. The days when having your picture taken was a mysterious or even fearful event had already passed, and sitting for the photographer had become a common experience. As such, the tension and creativity that initially attended the ritual gave way to a voluminous studio production of images in which subjects posed routinely before fixed backdrops. Criticizing their commercial-studio counterparts for their lack of creativity, amateur photographers looked to landscape photography to provide an alternative, and portrait photography came to be considered passe.

The above was not the only reason art photographers chose landscapes as their subject. Being amateurs, they viewed photography as an private hobby: only a small percentage regarded their own work and that of their peers with a critical eye, or embraced the medium as a means for plumbing ideals of beauty and the meaning of existence. For most, photography was a convenient diversion, a means for balming egos bruised by the vicissitudes of "modern life." The waterside landscape—the paradigmatic theme of *art photography* then, usually shot in soft-focus so as to blur the distinction between foreground and background—can be seen as a projection of the momentary sense of peace so sought after by these practitioners.

Viewed in this context, Nojima's portraits evince a gravity of gaze—directed within and without—that had no equal. Far from being a hobby, photography was for Nojima a goal to be approached with utmost seriousness—one that had the potential to consume the self. And it is for this reason that Nojima's work sometimes strikes us as a quest not for beauty, but for morality.

Looking at his portraits, one feels Nojima's kinship more with late-Tokugawa and early-Meiji photographs and *yoga* (Western-style) painters like Matsusaburo Yokoyama and Yuichi Takahashi, than with his contemporaries. When photographic technique first came to Japan in the 1850s, few made the distinction between photography and *yoga*: With their powers to represent reality as it is, both of these arts stunned the Japanese. Yokoyama ran a photography studio at Ueno Ikenohata and a *yoga* school called Tsutenro, and Takahashi made some paintings based directly on landscape photographs. Eclipsing the boundaries between photography and *yoga*, these two artists became obsessed with this *mirror* which—more faithfully than anything else—reflected the world before their eyes.

The mirror not only revealed the environment that unfolded before them, but their own presence within this reality as well. With the advent of the mirrors of photography and *yoga*, representations of the self (and consequently of one's inner life) that were informed by depth and clarity rose vividly to the surface. Both Yokoyama and Takahashi were known also for their self-portraits. Using both painting and photography Yokoyama continued to make self-portraits from his youth to his later years. Discovering oneself led to an understanding of others. One's gaze extended to another and groped to read the contours it found there—the idea of the modern portrait as an expressive means for defining presences discrete from one's own continued to grow during this time.

Nojima sought to faithfully retrace the process through which the pioneers of the late-Tokugawa and early-Meiji periods evolved the notion of the portrait. In the same way that Ryusei Kishida abandoned post-Impressionism to work his way backwards along the lineage of representation, Nojima aimed to recover the shock of encounter with the real that the portrait photography of these two ages afforded. The secret (though not the only one) behind the power of Nojima's work is that when viewing his portraits we are assaulted by the simple (hence archetypal) feeling that *that person is there.*

In my earlier writing, *Gyoshi Suru Seishin—Nojima Yasuzo Ron* (The Gaze of the Mind—Yasuzo Nojima) (1986), I have commented that his photography can be divided into two separate periods: the first from 1920 to 1923, the second from 1930 to 1933. Between the two periods there are subtle differences in the style of his portraits and other photographs of people. Since the early works were printed using gumbichromate, their compositions are informed by a quiet classical atmosphere. Since his subjects in these works sat absolutely still while gazing back at the camera, their personalities resonated with authority in the resulting image. These images reflected the deep influence Nojima received from the writers and painters of the *Shirakaba* (White Birch) school and show him in pursuit of *the revelation of individuality.* In *Shusetsu Zakki* (Scarlet Snow Notes)(1920), he wrote: "I carry on my inner life through photography." His portraits during this time are suffused with tension, for despite their still-as-death exteriors, we see in them the shower of sparks that fly between the self and the other.

In the latter works he adds another element to this moral dimension. In *Jinbutsu Sakugaho* (Portraying The Figure, 1927)—the only text that he wrote regarding his portraiture—Nojima discusses "the perception of chiaroscuro and form," and the "the pleasure of making: "

> When making portraits, I move the subject to a place with suitable light and first just look. Then I evaluate the qualities of light and shadow and of form. Once I am pleased, I immediately shoot. I am not concerned with capturing the model's personality or revealing his or her special attributes. I shoot in accordance my perceptions of light and form: these elements hold with my interest. ....While some photographs embrace the look of the model and attempt to exploit the feeling inherent in this look, I am not capable of this. I am more attracted to the joys of composition. At any rate, I cannot but be guided by my perceptions.

What held Nojima's interest was not the model's character but the plastic beauty of form and proportion. What determined the composition and content of his portraits were his perceptions of light and form. The stability introduced by placing the face in the center of the frame and the gravity of the subject's character—both qualities of the earlier Taisho era works—give way here to a frozen flash of grace. The picture plane becomes invested with dynamism—and Nojima carries out bold experiments like cutting faces in half (as in *Hosokawa Chikako*) or creating montages with multiple-exposures.

There is no doubt that the changes seen in these latter portraits were inspired by the *new photography* of the 1930s. "This German-born movement in photography" (Ihee Kimura)

affected Nojima more than it did any other Japanese photographer. While the results of his pursuit of *perception* were compositionally dazzling, they evoked fashion photography devoid of content. His best efforts, however, were reproduced in the magazine *Koga* (Light Pictures) (1932–33), and his close-up portraits of women were shown in his exhibition *Photographs of Women's Faces—20 Pieces*, at the Kinokuniya Gallery in Ginza (1933).

Looking again at Nojima's portraits, I realize that in addition to the direct influence of the *new photography* on the compositions of his later works, there are definitive differences between the Taisho-era works and the later photographs. One of these contrasts centers on why, in the works from the 1930s, Nojima became so engrossed with photographing women. Excluding rare exceptions like *Koreya Senda*, almost all of the images Nojima showed in *Koga* and at his Ginza exhibition were of anonymous female models. In particular, he demonstrated a singular attachment to the woman whose image appeared on the first photo-page of the inaugural issue of *Koga* (March, 1932): "Model F." He left a surprising number of both portraits of her face and full-nudes. We can only assume that through her intense gaze at the camera, her untamed almost impudent expression, and her thick and heavy body, "Model F" personified Nojima's ideal woman.

In tracing a wide spectrum of expressions and gestures of unnamed female models, the works from the 1930s contrast directly with the male images that predominate in the Taisho photographs. The models for these earlier works were men of culture like Muneyoshi Yanagi, Kazumasa Nakagawa, and Kenkichi Tomimoto (who also happened to be Nojima's friends). There were also anonymous male subjects in such works as *Portrait of Mr. S.* (1921)—a photograph of Nojima's houseboy—and *Boy with a Cold* (1920). For the most part, however, the subjects were men of firm social status who Nojima rendered with their personalities intact.

On the other hand, the female models in the later works are portrayed as nameless and without character. As exemplified by the tag "F." these models were treated as interchangeable symbols. In the Taisho work, individual subjects are each represented by a single work: in the 1930s work, the women—one capable of substituting for another—are repeatedly photographed as if under observation from a fixed vantage point.

The primary difference in cultural life between the Taisho-era days before the Great Kanto Earthquake and the 1920s and 1930s derives from the growth, in the latter, of the modern city. And what haunted the swiftly transforming, multi-faceted spaces of this new urban world was not the discrete face of the individual, but the faceless throng— the very crowd that would soon be mobilized for a state of war. Nojima seems to have scooped his female models from the center of this featureless mass of the modern city. As such, in contrast to proper names like Muneyoshi Yanagi and Koreya Senda, these models are indicated by signifiers like "F."

By virtue of their absence of idiosyncratic natures, these women become perfect vehicles for bearing the *Zeitgeist* of Tokyo in the 1930s: in "Model F.'s" brazenness, fleshy form, and expressions replete with sentiment, we see reflections of her place and time. With remarkable perseverance, Nojima delves into the changing face of woman to wrest from it a brief flash of the modern city.

To find such a woman as "Model F." from amidst the urban swarm is a measure of Nojima's peerless vision. And looking back to one of his earliest nudes, *Woman Leaning on a Tree* (1915), we discover a brilliant continuity to this vision. As if rooted, his women stand steadfastly, examples of the image that Nojima constantly pursued : that of the "earth mother." In the images of "Model F." the mad brilliance of the modern metropolis, a stormy eroticism, and the earthy aroma of *gaia*, are all powerfully lashed together. In evoking the whole strata of Nojima's imagery in single photographs, these pictures narrate the power of his portraiture.

Unfortunately, the period during which Nojima produced these unforgettable photographic portraits was not long. Prone to illness, his poor health robbed him of the concentration he needed to work. And when Japan became a country at war in the 1940s, it was virtually impossible for photographers to freely carry on their work. Though Nojima lived until 1964, he produced few noteworthy works in his latter years.

Now that the genre of portrait photography has been thoroughly dismantled, Nojima's works may seem antiquated. But when I look at them I feel a peculiar rush of excitement and emotion, these ostensibly "flat" images begin to heave and swell with raw vitality. While reactions to his images may vary according to individual and generation, the simple and primary feeling that *that person is there* is something that will not easily fade. (translated by Charles Worthen)

Nojima's Portraits of Nudes

Yuri Mitsuda
assistant curator, The Shoto Museum of Art

1———Yasuo Nojima and *Nude Torso*

Slightly twisted at the waist, with breasts uplifted, stands the model's polished body in *Nude Torso* (1930, Pl. 45). Her black undergarment, on the verge of coming undone just below her tight waist, echoes the rich cascade of her black hair. The process of substituting the features of her face for a simple form heightens the image's sensuality, Her body is both innocent and sturdy. The post on the left and the round handle of the sliding door on the right confine the wilderness of her flesh in a cramped Japanese interior ; the essence of the Japanese woman — a solid beauty neither traditional nor modern — pervades the space.

Within the deep texture of this scrupulously executed bromoil image, Nojima delineates the reality of Japanese feminine beauty. Its simple though taut geometries of composition and volume are crystallizations of Nojima's modernist awareness of the plastic arts. The brilliant fruition of Nojima's notion of the *beauty of perception* is a measure of an intellect that sought to both fathom and affirm the quality of Japanese life at that time.

In a modern Japan hell-bent to Westernize itself, using an imported camera and working with a medium that was invented much later than painting, Nojima produced his singular images.

After entering Japan at about the same time as *yoga* (Western oil-painting), photography was first studied as an advanced form of Western scientific technology. While Japanese people were stunned by the fresh sense of the real evinced by both photography and yoga, Japanese *yoga* painters did not — unlike painters in the West — react to the former with a mixture of dread and curiosity. This ironically enabled people here to view photography as both a simple technique and no different from oil painting (an impossibility for Europeans with their long tradition of painting). In the unusual climate of Japanese modernism, photography-as-art got off to a late start.

It was not until the Meiji period that people began to consider photography as a means for expression. This fresh role for the medium was taken up not by commercial-studio photographers (who were merely seen as technicians), but by amateurs in love with a new (and expensive) hobby. They formed salon-like associations. Nojima did much of his work at the *Tokyo Shashin Kenkyo Kai* (Tokyo Photography Study Group), founded in 1907 and one of the oldest organizations. Nojima began his work as an artist at around the same time these groups started their awkward attempts at "expression." That the groups' search for models led them to *nihonga* (Japanese painting) and *yoga* is only natural. Initially, their works — which came to be know as *geijutsu shashin* ("art photographs") — were sentimental products based on *nihonga*. While most of these amateurs were rightly oriticized for creating works based on a convenient hireling aesthetic and thereby devoid of artistic merit, there were members whose deep contemplation of nature led them to acts of expressive power.[1] And from our perspective today, attacking photography solely on the grounds that it borrowed painting's aesthetic seems simplistic. In light of the following passage through the *shinko shashin* ("new photography") of Germany to the news photograph that understanding of "art photograph" can be viewed as a temporary stage in the course of an ever-changing medium.

Yasuzo Nojima was a superlative artist. For his subjects, he plumbed the very depths of their existence, and seeking a personal aesthetic that was neither conventional nor borrowed, arrived at carefully crafted art that brimmed with spiritual meaning. For the sake of contrast we have included in this exhibition the finest paintings of his contemporaries, Ryusei Kishida, Ryuzaburo Umehara, Tetsugoro Yorozu, and Kazumasa Nakagawa. Following his own course, always a few years behind these painters, Nojima was not a pathfinder, but nevertheless realized his unique vision.

Nojima did not view painting only through the prism of his medium ; he saw painting as painting and photography as photography ; being a *man who saw*, Nojima had a unsurpassed knowledge of the art of his day. For Kishida and the others, their friend Nojima wore many hats ; he was both patron and collector ; he planned their exhibitions, photographed their works, and interpreted their art through his activities. As such, his photography must be seen in context with these other important pursuits.

The issues that artists contended with then — painting vs photograghy, East vs West, and technique vs expression — seemed to have all at once quietly fused within Nojima. Happily, the passive nature of photography dovetailed with the temperament of this *man who saw*.[2] Add to this combination the yearnings of an individual living in a modern Japanese society which continually sought to absorb and interpret things Western.

While the issues above may have faded somewhat in the interim, thcy remain unsolved. Since rabid consumerism today has relegated photography to the nested boxes of the simulacra, Nojima's pictures have a particularly independent and fresh psychological appeal ; they make possible a renewed critique on the power of the image.

2———Early Nudes & *Woman Leaning on a Tree*

Though Yasuzo Nojima lived for 75 years, the period in which he produced his best work was short. Moreover, out of all of the works what he made, only 259 have been "discovered." Though we have only these work to judge his achievement, it is clear that the most remarkable photographs of his oeuvre were born during two extremely brief periods, 1915-23 and 1930-33. Prominent among both series of images were his portraits of nudes.

Since the 1930 date recorded for the powerful image *Nude Torso* refers to the year the work was printed, it may have been taken much earlier. Nojima frequently printed film long after shooting it, and many of the works between 1914-23 were of bare-chested women, the lower halves of whose bodies were cloaked.

The 1914 work *Woman Combing Her Hair (pl. 4)* employs the traditional pose of the woman making her toilet. That the language of her body comes to us not through shading, but via a delicate retouching of her contours, betrays the sway *ukiyoe* prints still held over Nojima. The same influence is apparent in works made until 1920, like *Standing Woman* (1917, pl.7). And with its thickly rendered contours and suppression of the volumetric, *Woman* (1918, pl. 8) is a clear example of the aesthetics of *nihonga*.

In as much as these images portray women in the everyday activities of making up and dressing, they go no further than the traditional genre pictures which existed until the Meiji period.[3] With their blank faces and averted glances, these women are powerless and passive, and even seem unaware of their being photographed.

There is, however, one work that does not fit in this category: *Woman Leaning on a Tree* (1915, pl. 5). While the outlines may stiffen, the bold seminude woman resting one hand on the trunk of a tree and standing firmly upon the ground, is rendered with gravity. Though "the beauty beneath the tree," which originated in Indian art, is a composition that exists in both the East and West, here she is worlds apart from her predecessors.

While the wisteria trellis in the background alerts us that we are in a garden, we sense that the woman and the tree are directly rooted not to their surroudings but to the ground itself. This image of tree of life and steady bare-breasted *earth mother* recalls Ryusei Kishida's *Woman with a Squash* (1914, pl. 111). Though Kishida painted few nudes, some of them derive from the image of the Virgin Mary and portray gentle and motherly women.[4] Through its folkloric quality and evocation of a farming woman, *Woman with a Squash* is an exception to these others.

Throughout the Meiji period, *yoga* nudes were either paintings of Western women — hence imbued with a European aesthetic — or versions of traditional Japanese genre pictures; Tetsugoro Yorozu's powerful 1912 work, *Naked Beauty* (fig. 1), was the first painting to break from these conventions. While the work does relate to Gauguin's paintings of Tahitian women (which were well-known at the time), the revelation of the aggressive (as opposed to sexual) presence of the reclining seminude woman was indicative of a revolutionary artistic consciousness. In the world of Japanese photography, most nudes had appeared as pitiful creatures captured in secret — a la the works found in *Meiji Nude Photography* — and it was not until Nojima's *Woman Leaning on a Tree* that there existed any images equipped with intrinsic expressive power. As such, Yorozu and Nojima can be viewed as contemporaries in search of a common aesthetic.

As has often been said, Nojima preferred full-bodied models, and it cannot be denied that there existed within him an underlying yearning for robust and motherly women.

Not all of his nude portraits, however, express this all-encompassing sacred maternality. For Nojima, his defiant *Woman Leaning on a Tree* has an aggressive and heterogeneous presence: an individual who represents and asserts the force of life. The distinctive feature that was to thread its way through all of his portraits of women is already clearly present in this photograph. Nojima appreciated women not so much for their individualities or personalities as for their ability to embody the life-force, to become vessels of a divine sensuality.

With her accentuated eyes, the model in *Woman Leaning on a Tree* stares right at us; she was the first of Nojima's subjects to directly return the gaze of his lens. With the exception of his portrait *Boy with a Cold* (1920, pl. 13), all of the artist's portraits between 1915–23 (which were mostly of men) were balanced compositions in which the subject avoided looking at the camera. Within each portrait of men, the faces — purged of sentiment and gesture — are replete with inner mysteries, and the pictures are suffused with a stern dignity.

Nojima must have had high regard for Ryusei Kishida's paintings in the middle of the 1910s; he went through troubles to purchase Kishida's *Portrait of Masamitsu Kawabata* (1918, pl. 110). The idealistic style invested in Kishida's portraits had an undeniable influence on Nojima. In addition to Kishida's idealism, Nojima's long-held belief that "representation was the main road to art" (which was supported by his reverence for the subject as a force of nature) was vital to his personal ideology. It is curious that despite regular visits to the photo studio to commemorate every special occasion, Kishida, on the other hand, remained completely indifferent to the connections between his painting — with its heightened realism — and photography. Though it is not pertinent here to discuss this in detail, Kishida's behavior in part points to the essential irony inherent in the relationship between modern Japanese painting and photography.[6]

At any rate, *Woman Leaning on a Tree* simultaneously diverges from Nojima's other early nudes by virtue of its fierce gaze of *the other* and embodies those elements which the artist continued to search for in his portraits of women. With its almost mythical affirmation of the potency of life, this image stood at the vanguard of the visual arts of its time.

3———The Interim Period

In Room 3 at the 1920 exhibition of the *Tokyo Shashin Kenkyu Kai* (Tokyo Photography Study Group), Nojima held a solo display of his works. During this event three of his nude portraits were removed by the police. Though thirty years had passed since a similar incident involving Seiki Kuroda's paintings of nudes, the Japanese public was apparently not ready for the open display of nude photographs. There were few exhibitions of nude photography in those days: models were difficult to find, and in the images that were displayed the women rarely revealed their faces. After *Woman Leaning on a Tree* even Nojima himself waited long to experiment again with photographing the nude outdoors. The age was simply not prepared for such works.

In a work made in the following year (1921) Nojima photographed a woman model in a pose similar a life-drawing model. The results: the model is stiff and the work remains merely a study.

4———The Nude Series from 1930–1931

Nojima's work with the nude reached its peak with his series in 1931 — a year that was a great turning point. The next year, Nojima's interest in *shinko shashin* grows stronger and he shifts to the style that would characterize his later works. As I will discuss later on, his subjects become fragmented, and are treated more colloquially and ephemerally. In 1931, Nojima's awareness of the medium's plastic potential and his understanding of form and volume sharpen, and at the same time his skills of observation engineer a melting together of his reverence for nature-as-life-force with his hidden eroticism. Through gradations of light, the touch of the mysterious flesh takes shape as "a thick and beautiful swelling surface."[7] And it is this rich texture — which is completely autonomous from oil painting — that sustains Nojima's photographs as works of art. The bromoil process which Nojima used during this fecund year allowed for delicate and sumptuous gradations of light. Here these tones blend —at the deepest level within the mind of the viewer — with the uncanny sensuality which the flesh emits.

In this series, Nojima employed folding screens in the background. The screen not only funtioned as a tool for subtly controlling light, it also simplified the background and consolidated the composition via its narrow perpendicular lines. Almost filling the picture plane — like ones in *Bushukan* (1930, pl. 28) — the nudes are sealed within compact quarters, which conversely yields an infinite spatial-temporal environment ; the spaces have a condensed presence which cultivates a keen tactility.

One nude gazes into a basin of water, another into a mirror ; isolated, they sink into the world of their own physical presence. Though these nudes, like Nojima's *Bushukan* and *Loquats*, are flung out into the harsh world, their inner life-energy remains undiminished. Here, neither motherly nor aggressive, they each stand as individual units of this energy ; boldly absorbing an erotic aura.

Among these images, two in which the model's faces are obscured (pls. 48, 51) have particular expressive strength. These two nudes are a study in opposites : one is characterized by centripetal silence, the other by centrifugal movement. While other works from this period have already begun to quote from *shinko shashin* via their emphasis of momentary expressions and gestures, these two images evince a drastic curtailment of incident ; as such, they represent of highly purified form of Nojima's idiosyncratic style.

The two images of the nudes with hidden faces are purged of detail, abstracted, and flee from the notion of photography as referent of the real. Nojima's first experience of the abstract presence of the nude-as-other must have been profoundly moving. These women are all independent others, each equipped with uncanny eros. They are no longer motherly. And though they are treated as solid forms, they never become mere objectsyet. During this brief interval, Nojima was able to produce an absolutely original version of the nude.

Nojima's remarks that "we must aspire to the beauty which we are given," and that "the job is to invest the subject with life through the manipulation of form and light and shadow," are most applicable to the two nudes discussed above. During this time Nojima wrote of photography and artmaking in his notebook titled "Fictions & True Stories," "If an artist fails to weave his intent and feelings into his art it will remain still-born. The resulting photograph will be merely didactic." Perhaps what he means by "fiction" is the method of creation —based on a discovery of the real — that invigorates one's "true stories." For such a profound *seer* as Nojima, this method became the unity of photography with art.

On the road to his singular vision of the nude, Nojima became attracted to and studied the nude portraits of the painter Ryuzaburo Umehara. The painter's examples of women sitting in relaxed poses or looking into mirrors seem to have worked their way into Nojima's photographs. Nojima, who chose to study painting under Umehara, was influenced by the painter's formidable nudes, by the thick reds and greens and bold contours of works in oil like *Nude* (1929).

While under the tutelage of Renoir in France, Umehara created paintings of soft and sensual women, and upon his arrival back in Japan he was forced — like so many other artists returning from abroad — to confront the perplexing issue of *Japanese* oil painting. Apparently, Nojima met Umehara two years after his return, and their friendship took place when the painter reached his fullest maturation. Umehara usally rendered the body in full, eschewing techniques of collage or fragmentation in order to arrive at the strong and voluptuous essence of his models. These works no doubt fascinated Nojima. And Nojima's fondness for the nude statue by Maillol that he received from Umehara was another indication of their like-minded inclinations.

Combining Momoyama-period ornamentality with thick-bodied Japanese women, Umehara pioneered, via his paintings, an exhaustive investigation in praise of the female form. In order to create his own version of *Japanese* oil painting, Umehara mined the richly expressive vein that has historically flowed through Japanese merchant culture. On the other hand, Nojima's work went in the opposite direction from Umehara's magnificent opulence to search for inner truths in simple forms, and to evoke the spiritual over the material. While Nojima's nudes preserved their folkloric audacity, they came to evince a more and more purified semblance of the life-force he strove to define.

Nojima assimilated and — through his continued cultivation of the bromoil print — competed with the oil-painting of the time, and his nudes from 1931 (just before his plunge into modernism) show him at work refining his notions of the *beauty of perception* via recent plastic conventions ; this rare body of work stands as a crystallization of the artist's deep respect for nature-as-life.

5——Nojima and Modernism

The composition of *Nude Torso* shares much with that of Koshiro Onchi's painting *After Bathing* (1928, fig. 2). Other than Onchi's 1920 one-person exhibition at Kabutoya, little is know of the relationship between the photographer and Onchi. We know, however, that Onchi did make photographs and included one, inspired by *shinko shashin,* called *Soaring Sensuality* (1934), illustrated a volume of his poetry.

Through his singular style, Onchi absorbed modernism to a much greater degree than Nojima. Creator of many abstract works and prominently influenced by expressionism, cubism, and futurism, Onchi deployed his motif of the human figure not as an integrated whole but as a form capable of being cleaved into parts. In that he dismantled his nudes geometrically and reconstituted them as iterations of these individual components, we can assume that he apprehended his subjects through the prism of *shinko shashin.*

Nojima's interest in the figure-as geometry (as hinted at in *Nude Torso*) rapidly intensifies in 1931. Works that portray portions of the figure, like *Title Unknown* (1931, pl. 28) predominate. Gradually the raw incompleteness of form revealed in this work, mutates into a fetishistic rendering of the leg as an object, as in *Still Life* (pl. 95). In images like the latter, the naturalism embodied in earlier statements by Nojima such as, "It is vital to capture nature at her most lively,"[9] is nowhere to be found.

It is during this time that Nojima plunged headlong into *shinko shashin.* He wrote the following in his journal:

> What they call "art photography" is nothing more than a catalog of the absentminded, the vague, the falsely significant or deep, the diluted, and the weak. There are, however, not the qualities the age demands.[10]

He then forsook the bromoil print for the sharpness of the gelatinesilver print. His own disavowal of "that world of feeble sweetness,"[11] (mentioned in one of his notebooks) may be interpreted as the artist's negation of his earlier work. In answer to social conditions of the time and to the introduction of a German aesthetic in the Japanese artworld, Nojima added words like *science, functionalism, machinery,* and *technology* to his expressive vocabulary.

Enter the Western dress-clad, bobbed-haired, pleasure-seeking model. Nojima photographed these models in high heels, smoking cigarettes, draped in feather boas, thereby concealing the primary dignity of their bodies. In modern interiors with striped carpets, they smile blankly. Here, Nojima pours his expressive energies into the superficial transience of popular culture, and we cannot help but feel that something of his has been destroyed.

Nojima's transmogrification (described by Mr. Toshiharu Itoh as his "discovery of the urban woman") exposes not only the artist's attempts to cope with the sudden modernization and urbanization of Japanese society, but also the tremendous rift these changes brought about in Japanese history.[12] From its inaugural issue, the magazine *Koga* (Light Pictures) served as a forum for Nojima's remarkable images of women's faces. After this series was completed, however, Nojima's work rapidly deteriorated, and his singular aesthetic vanished.

In another notebook entry, he wrote: "Just because I am Japanese does not mean that I have to make 'Japanese' art." We can only wonder how Nojima viewed Umehara's ever-more pronounced interest in "Japanese" painting, Yorozu's embrace of Southern Chinese painting, and the early-declining Kishida's involvement with Sogen painting. Nojima hardly ever travelled abroad, and though the above quote is all we know of his attitude towards his Japanese identity, that he gradually became estranged from these painters seems no mere coincidence. The series of empty experiments that led to the diminution of both the quality and quantity of his art was emblematic of a great renouncement in Nojima's life, one that points to a host of questions left for us to resolve.

(translated by Charles Worthen)

(1) Refer to the works of Shinzo Fukuhara, Hakuyo Fuchigami, Masataka Takayama, and Chotaro Hidaka.
(2) Refer to *Yazuzo Nojima — A Clarity of Vision,* also published in this catalog.
(3) Kikuo Miyashita, "Changing Views of the Nude," *Sansai,* (October-November 1990).
(4) This vision of the Virgin Mary is most prominent in Ryusei Kishida's *Eternal Idol* (1914).
(5) *Meiji Nude Photography,* Yuko Shobo (1970). This book is a collection of images sold as pornography and photographs of prostitutes.
(6) Ryusei Kishida left behind a tremendous number of commemorative photographs and portraits. His albums also contain several photographs which he took. In his theories on art, however, he never discussed photography. I am indebted to Mr. Tohru Asano for his suggestions regarding this matter.
(7) Words from Nojima's correspondence as quoted in Seison Yamazaki's article "The Works of Yasuo Nojima," *Shashin Geppo* (April, 1920).
(8) Ryuzaburo Umehara, "Remembering Yasuzo Nojima, "*The Memorial Exhibition for Yasuzo Nojima* (1965).
(9) Yasuzo Nojima, "Portraying the Figure," *Ars Shashin Daikoza* (1929).
(10) Quoted from Nojima's notebook. All quotes are taken from the same notebook which is believed to have been written between 1932-1933.
(11) Ibid.
(12) Toshiharu Itoh, "Discovery of the Urban Woman," *Camera Mainichi* (June, 1983).

野島康三略年譜

1889 2月12日埼玉県浦和市に生まれる。父は中井銀行頭取。

1904 慶応義塾大学普通部に入学

1906 この頃から独習で写真を始める

1907 東京写真研究会との交流が始まる

1909 東京写真研究会主催による第2回写真品評会に出品
慶応義塾大学経済学部に入学

1910 東京写真研究会に入会、第1回東京写真研究会展に出品

1911 健康を害し慶応義塾大学を中退する

1911-12 小野隆太郎、山崎静村、山本義雄と四人会を結成する。この頃まで野島熙正の名で作品を発表する

1912 第3回東京写真研究会展で《にごれる海》(1910、Pl.1)二等賞を授賞する

1912-14 フュウザン会(1912-13)、二科会(1914-　)の画家たちとの交流が始まる

1915 人形町に三笠写真店を開設、草土社(1915-22)の作家たちとの交流が始まる

1918 日本創作版画協会の設立とその活動に援助を与える

1919-20 神田神保町に兎屋畫堂を開設、フュウザン会、二科会、草土社、創作版画協会系の作家の作品を展示する(*開催展覧会記録の項を参照)

1920 東京写真研究会の第10回研展会場(上野竹之台陳列館)の第3室で個展を開催裸婦作品3点が撤去される(写真30点;『写真月報』1920年2月号に作品目録が掲載される)
三笠写真店と兎屋畫堂を閉じ、新たに九段に野々宮写真館を開設する

1922 春陽会の設立メンバーとなり、春陽会展に油彩画を出品する。小石川竹早町の自宅野島邸で岸田劉生、萬鐵五郎、梅原龍三郎などの個展を開催する(*展覧会記録の項を参照)。野島邸での展覧会の展評が「中央美術」などに掲載される。

1924 父が死去

1925 国画創作協会の第二部(洋画)創設に関与し、翌年の第1回展に油彩画を出品、国画会会友に推挙される

1928 国画創作協会第一部解散、第二部の国画会としての発足に伴い、川路柳虹、福原信三らと同会評議員となる
福原信三らと絵画主義写真を主張する日本写真会の創立に参加、会員となる

1930 柳宗悦らの日本民芸館の設立運動に協力、設立委員となる。野島邸で浜田庄司、富本憲吉らの個展を開催
中山岩太、ハナヤ勘兵衛らが設立した芦屋カメラクラブの同人に推挙される

1931 朝日新聞社が主催し東京(4月)、大阪(7月)で開催された「独逸国際移動写真展」から大きな影響を受ける。この頃から印画技法も近代的なゼラチンシルバー・プリントに変える

fig.10:兎屋畫堂披露宴／1919年3月29日

1932-33 伊那信男、木村伊兵衛、中山岩太らと写真雑誌『光画』を創刊、出版資金の大部分を援助する。『光画』は新興写真の運動に大きな影響を与えた。同誌のブック・デザインとタイポグラフィはデザイナーの原弘が担当した

1933 銀座紀伊国屋で個展「野島康三作:写真女の顔・20点」を開催、同展の展示は原弘によってデザインされた

1934 銀座三昧堂で個展

1935 アシヤ写真サロンの同人になる。慶応義塾大学カメラクラブ顧問、全日本写真連盟委員に就任

1939 福原信三と共に国画会写真部を創設

1952 第二回「写真の日」に日本写真協会より表彰される

1954 国画会制度改革に伴い、同会客員に推挙される

1963 日本フォトセンター相談役に就任

1964 8月14日葉山にて永眠、75歳。11月、東京の富士フォト・サロンで「野島康三回顧展」が開催される

1965 『野島康三遺作集』が刊行される。国展に「野島賞」が設定される

1971 1月18日、「野島康三氏と雑誌『光画』をしのぶ会」が東京有楽町バーシャンタンで行なわれる。11月、新宿ニコン・サロンで約40点の作品による個展が開催される。

1975 9月、ハナヤ勘兵衛によって大阪の彼のスタジオで「日本近代写真の夜明け:野島康三」展が開催される

1976 5月、東京の喜怒哀楽コレクション・ギャラリーで個展が開催される。

1978 10月、東京都美術館の「写真と絵画」展に作品が出品される

1979 5月、シカゴのギルバート・ギャラリーで個展が開催される。シカゴ・トリビューン紙、シカゴ・サンタイム紙などに「日本のスティーグリッツを発見…」として大きく取りあげられる。8-9月、イリノイ州バタビアで開催された原子物理学者国際会議の

会期中、フエルミ・ナショナル加速機研究所付属ギャラリーで個展を開催。ノーベル賞受賞者レオン・リーダーマン所長の紹介文を添えたパンフレットが発行される

1981 野島康三写真作品148点が、作品の保存上の処置と専門的調査を受けるためにシカゴ美術館に寄託される

1982 シカゴ美術館写真部設立記念の「シカゴ美術館所蔵写真展」に作品が出品される。展覧会カタログに作品図版収録

1984 10月、大阪の国立国際美術館で開催の「芸術としての写真:その誕生から今日まで―シカゴ美術館のコレクションから―」に野島作品5点が出品される。

1986 パリ、ポンピドゥ・センター国立近代美術館で開催の「前衛の日本」展に14点の作品が出品される

1988 野島康三写真作品148点がシカゴ美術館から返還され、京都国立近代美術館に寄託される。東京都美術館で開催され山口県立近代美術館、兵庫県立近代美術館を巡回した、「1920年代展」に作品が出品される。神奈川県立近代美術館で開催の「1930年代の日本の写真」に作品が出品される

1989 ワシントンのナショナル・ギャラリー・オブ・アート(5-7月)とシカゴ美術館(9-11月)、ロサンゼルス・カウンティ美術館(12-1990年1月)で開催された「オン・ザ・アート・オブ・フィキシング・シャドウ:写真の150年」展に作品が出品される。11月、東京の有楽町朝日ギャラリーで開催された「『光画』とその時代―1930年代の新興写真」展に作品20点が出品される

1990 11月、パリのパレ・ド・トウキョウでビエンナーレ形式で開催される〈写真月間〉の「絵画主義からモダニズムへ」展に作品が50点が出品される
『光画』復刻版が発行される

1991 渋谷区立松濤美術館と京都国立近代美術館で「野島康三とその周辺」展が開催される

YASUZO NOJIMA CHRONOLOGY

1889 Born February 12, at Urawa City, outside of Tokyo. Father is an executive of the Nakai Bank.

1904 Enters the lower school of Kcio Gijiku University in Tokyo.

1906 Starts to photograph.

1907 Nojima submits early photographs to the *Tokyo Shashin Kenkyukai* [Tokyo Photography Study Group, 1907-present]

1909 Included in the second *Shashin Hinpyokai* [Juried Exhibiton of Photography] sponsored by the Tokyo Shashin Kenkyukai.
Enters the College of Economics [*Rizaibu*] at Keio University.

1910 Becomes an official member of the Tokyo Shashin Kenkyukai and is included in their first exhibit.

1911 Leaves Keio University due to poor health.

1911-12 *Yoninkai* [The Group of Four] Nojima, Ono Ryotaro, Yamazaki Seison, and Yamamoto Yoshio. The Yoninkai members may have exhibited together at Takamura Kotaro's gallery "Rokando" following Ono's one man show there during this period.

1912 *Fusainkai* [Charcoal Sketch Association 1912-1913] Among the first independent associations of modern artists.

1914 *Nikakai* [Second Division Group, 1914-present] An important modern artists association founded in opposition to government-sponsored Bunten.

1915 Nojima opens the *Mikasa Shashin Ten* [Mikasa Photo Shop, 1915-1920] in the Ningyo Cho district of Tokyo.
Sodosha [Grass and Earth Society, 1915-1922]

1918 *Kokuga Sosaku Kyokai* [The Association for the Creation of a New National Style of Painting. 1918-1928]
Nihon Sosaku Hanga Kyokai [Japan Original Print Association, 1918-1931, reorganized as Nihon Hanga Kyokai, 1931-present]

1919-20 Nojima opens gallery *Kabutoya Gado* in the Jimbo-Cho district of Tokyo, and exhibits artists from; *Fusainkai, Nikakai, Sodosha,* and *Sosaku Hanga Kyokai.* Kabutoya Gado exhibits include:
1919: March 29, Inauguration Party; May 3-4, "Invitational Assembly: Contemporary Domestic Artists in Western-style Painting, Sculpture, Artistic Crafts"; June 1-25, "Upcoming Western-style Artists Exhibition Of New Works" (Artists: Hazama Inosuke, Sekine Shoji, Nabei Kat-

suyuki, Yasuda Ryumon, Hayashi Shizue, Yamazaki Shozo); August 1 -25, "Drawing Exhibition"(Artists: Kawakami Ryoka, Oda Kazuma, Morita Tsunetomo, Sakamoto Hanjiro, Umehara Ryuzaburo, Saito Yori, Ishii Kakuzo, Yamazaki Shozo, Nabei Katsuyuki, Yasuda Ryumon, Nakahara Teijiro); September 2-25, "Sekine Shoji Posthumous Exhibition"; September 28-October 6, "Juried Exhibition of Western-style Painting," Jurors: Yasui Sataro, Umehara Ryuzaburo, Saito Yori; 8-17, "Oda Kazuma"; October 21-November 9, "Soshoku Bijutsuka Kyokai" ["Ornamental Artists Society"]; November 11-30, "Muraymama Kaita Posthumous Exhibition."
1920: January. 9-10, "Reproductions of Water colors by Rodin"; January 20-31, "Ishii Kakuzo"; February 18-29, "Childrens Free Painting Exhibition" Selected by: Yamamoto Kanae, Ishii Kakuzo, Nagahara Kotaro; March 2-15, "Nabei Katsuyuki"; March 16-31, "Hayashi Shizue"; April 1-15, "Nakagawa Kazumasa"; April 17-30, "Hazama Inosuke"; May 2-10, "Onchi Koshiro"; May 13-23, "Oomori Shoji, Drawings"; May 25 -30, "Umehara Ryuzaburo"; May 26-30, "Yamazaki Shozo"; June 2-5, "Koyama Keizo." In addition to the listed exhibits a variety of other works were informally shown.

1920 One man show at the annual Tokyo Shashin Kenkyukai exhibit (30 pieces). Reviewed in magazines Shashin Geppo (Tokyo: Konishiroku, February, 1920).
Nojima sells Mikasa Shashin Ten and closes Kabutoya Gado.
Opens *Nonomiya Shashin Kan* [Nonomiya Photography Studio]

1922 Shunyokai [Spring Society, 1922-present] Nojima becomes founding member and exhibits his paintings in their annual salons.
Nojima Tei [Nojima Salon] During this period Nojima sponsored a series of important exhibitions in his home. These exhibits were announced and reviewed in various newspapers and art journals including *Shirakaba* and *Chuo Bijutsu.* From May 25-29, Nojima presented a one man exhibit for the painter Kishida Ryusei featuring oil portraits by Kishida of his daughter Reiko, a signal event in this period. Other exhibits include: July 8-10, Japanese-style painting by Yorozu Tetsugoro; October 1-3, Oil Paintings by Yokobori Kakujiro; December 2-4 Oil, Paintings by Kobayashi Tokusaburo; December 17-19, Ceramics by Tomimoto Kenkichi.

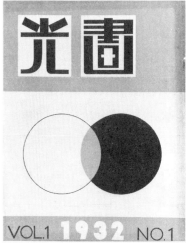

fig.11:『光画』創刊号 (Vol. 1, No. 1)／1932／資料6

fig.12:『光画』(Vol. 2, No. 1)／1933／資料6

1924 Father dies.

1925 *Kokuga Sosaku Kyokai, Yoga-bu* [Western-style Painting Division of The Association for the Creation of a New National Style of Painting, 1925-1928] Nojima becomes a founding board member with Fukuhara Shinzo, Kawaji Pyuko, and Tanaka Kisaku. Exhibits his paintings in annual salons.
Marries Komiya Ineko.

1927 Builds villa in Karuizawa.

1928 Kokuga Sosaku Kyokai dissolved and the Yoga-bu reforms as Kokugakai [National Painting Association, 1928-present] Nojima becomes founding board member and exhibits his paintings in annual salons.
Nihon Shashin Kai [Japan Photographic Society, 1924-present] An influential pictorial photography organization based in Tokyo, founded by Fukuhara Shinzo. Nojima becomes a member.

1930 *Nihon Mingeikan* [Folk Craft Museum of Japan, initiated 1930, incorporated 1936-present] Founded by Yanagi Soetsu (Muneyoshi). Nojima becomes contributor.
Ashiya Camera Club founded by Nakayama Iwata, Hanaya Kanbei, and others. Nojima is close to this group and supports their efforts. (Their first exhibit, held in Kobe, included a selection of works by Man Ray.)

1931 Touring version of the exhibition *Film und Foto* sponsored in Japan by the Asahi Newspaper Group at Tokyo (May), then Osaka (July).

1932-33 Nojima sponsors and publishes *Koga* [Light Pictures] a journal which served to introduce the New Vision and New Objectivity movements from abroad, and became the major publication of the *Shinko Shashin* [New Photography] movement in Japan. Nojima, Kimura Ihee, Nakayama Iwata, and Ina Nobuo are principal members. Hara Hiromu contributes important articles on graphic design and typography. Nojima publishes his new photographs here.

1933 One man show [*Works by Nojima Yasuzo, Photographs of Women's Faces, 20 Pieces* at Kinokuniya Gallery in the Ginza district of Tokyo, with a novel exhibition plan by Hara Hiromu. Reviewed in *Koga*, vol. 2, 1933. p. 266.

1934 One man exhibition at the Sanmai Do gallery in the Ginza district of Tokyo.

1935 Ashiya Camera Club expands activities to sponsor annual juried exhibit *Ashiya Shashin Salon*. Nojima becomes member. Published annually in *Ashiya Salon* magazine (1935-1940).
Nojima becomes official advisor to Keio University Camera Club.
Zen Nihon Shashin Renmei [All Japan Photography League, 1926-present] Nojima becomes member.

1939 *Kokugakai Shashinbu* [Photography Division of the National Painting Association, 1939-present] Nojima becomes a founding board member with Fukuhara Shinzo. Exhibits in their annual salons.

1952 Won official commendation from Photographic Society of Japan, (1952-present) on their second "Photography Day".

1963 Nojima supports Park Studio papers of incorporation as an advisor to Japan Photo Center, Inc. (1964-1984, largest commercial studio in Japan).

1964 Dies after long illness August 14, 1964 at Hayama Ishiki, outside of Tokyo.
Memorial exhibition at Fuji Photo Salon, Ginza (November).

1965 Memorial Monograph published.

1971 One man exhibit at Shinjuku Nikon Salon (November). Nikon Club publishes catalog. 40 illustrations, text by Miki Jun.

1975 *The Dawn of Modern Japanese Photography, Nojima Yasuzo Photography Exhibit* organized by Hanaya Kanbei at his Sun Store Photo Salon, Osaka (September).

1976 One man exhibit at Kid Airaku Collection Gallerie, in Shibuya, Tokyo (May).

1978 Included in exhibit *Photography and Painting* at the Tokyo Metropolitan Art Museum, Ueno, Tokyo (October).

1979 One man exhibition, the Gilbert Gallery, Ltd., Chicago, Illinois (May). Reviews: Alan G. Artner, "Work of Japanese lensman is a Broadening development." *Chicago Tribune.* 11 May, 1979. David Elliott, "Gilbert Discovers the Stieglitz of Japan." *Chicago Suntimes,* 13 May, 1979.
One man exhibition at Fermi National Accelerator Laboratory Gallery, Batavia, Illinois, during International Conference of Nuclear Physicists (August-September). Pamphlet published, introduction by nobel prize winner Dr. Leon Lederman, Director of Fermilab.

1981 Photographs from the Nojima Collection loaned to The Art Institute of Chicago. Collection shown to curators, scholars, and guests.

1982 Included in *Photographs from Chicago Collections,* opening exhibition for the new Department of Photography at the Art Institute of Chicago. Catalog published.

1984 Included in *The Art of Photography Past and Present from the Art Institute of Chicago* at The National Museum of Art, Osaka. Catalog published.

1986 Included in *Japon Des Avant Gardes* at the Musée national d'art moderne, Centre Georges Pompidou, Paris (December). Catalog published including article *Nojima et l'avant-garde,* by Jeffrey Gilbert. 5 illustrations.

1988 The Nojima Collection returned to Japan and placed on extended loan to the National Museum of Modern Art, Kyoto.
Included in *The 1920's in Japan* at the Tokyo Metropolital Art Museum (April-June), then Yamaguchi Prefectural Museum of Art (July-August), and Hyogo Prefectural Museum of Art (October-November). Catalog published with 15 illustrations.
Introductory exhibition in the photography section of the permanent collection galleries at the National Museum of Modern Art, Kyoto (May-July). The museum's publication *Miru* (May, 1988) includes article Nojima Yasuzo's Art by Jeffrey Gilbert. 4 illustrations.
Included in *Japanese Photography in 1930s* at The Museum of Modern Art, Kamakura (September-October). Catalog published with 20 illustrations.

1989 Included in *On the Art of Fixing a Shadow : 150 Years of Photography* at the National Gallery of Art (May-July), The Art Institute of Chicago (September-November), Los Angeles County Museum of Art (December-February, 1990). Catalog published with 1 illustration.
Included in *Koga to Sono Jidai* at Asahi Kaikan, Tokyo (November). Catalog published with 22 illustrations.

1990 Included in *Kokugakai Exhibition* at Tokyo Metroporitan Museum (September), Catalog published. Included in *150 years of photography Exhibition* at Konica Plaza, Catalog Published.
Included in *Pictorialism to Modernism* at the Palais de Tokyo, Paris (November)January 1991). Exhibgition organized by the Mission du Patrimoine Photographique on the occasion of the biennial *Mois de la Photo,* Japan being the main there for 1990. Illustrated catalog published.

1991 Nojima and Contemporaries Exhibition at the Shoto Museum of Art in Tokyo (July - August) ; The National Museum of Modern Art, Kyoto (September-October), Catalog published

NOTE : Japanese names have been entered in the Japanese manner, last name first (i. e. Nojima Yasuzo).

(organized by Jeffrey Gilbert)

ACKNOWLEDGEMENTS

A wide variety of sources were consulted to produce this chronology. Special thanks go to Mr. Fujii Toshio from the *Nojima Yasuzo Isaku Hozonkai* [The Nojima Collection], Mr. Iizawa Kohtaro, photo-historian, and The National Museum of Modern Art, Kyoto. As in any ongoing research, this information is subject to change and revision. Inquiries, additions, and corrections will be sincerely appreciated.

fig.13

fig.14

fig.15

fig.13, 14, 15: 野島康三個展「写真・女の顔20点」
／紀伊国屋ギャラリー／1933

出品作家略歴

岸田劉生〔RYUSEI KISHIDA〕

1891年東京京橋区銀座に生まれる。1906年東京高等師範学校付属中学を中退。洗礼を受けて、熱心なクリスチャンとして活動。1908年白馬会葵橋洋画研究所に入所、外光派の作風を学ぶ。1912年武者小路実篤らをしり、白樺派の同人たちと交友。後期印象派の影響を受ける。同年ヒュウザン会を結成。デューラーなど北方ルネッサンスを研究しはじめ、多く肖像画を描く。1915年草土社を結成。風景を主に描いていたが、1916年頃から静物画に着手。1918年から娘麗子を描いた連作を多数制作。1920年頃より南画、日本画の研究を始めた。1922年野島康三邸で個展。関東大震災後京都に移居してからは肉筆浮世絵、宗・元の絵画などに深く傾倒する。1929年、満州旅行の帰途、徳山市で客死。文筆にもすぐれ、「美の本体」など著作多数。

中川一政〔KAZUMASA NAKAGAWA〕

1893年東京文京区西片町に生まれる。短歌、詩を「早稲田文学」などに発表し文学に傾倒する一方、1914年から油彩画を独学。同年巽画会に初入選。1915年岸田劉生をたずね、白樺派同人たちとも交友。同年の草土社結成に参加、二科展にも出品する。後期印象派、岸田の強い影響を受けるが、やがて強い筆致で独特の洒脱な叙情をたたえた画風を確立。風景をよく描く。1920年兜屋畫堂で初個展。1922年春陽会の創立に客員として参加。1937年津田青楓と墨人倶楽部を結成。1940年には石井鶴三らと邦画一如会を結成。晩年は文人的な境地ともいえる自在な筆使いで、駒ヶ岳、薔薇を描いた作品が多い。1991年東京で死去。書をよくし、文筆活動も生涯盛んに行った。「腹の虫」などの著書多数。

梅原龍三郎〔RYUZABURO UMEHARA〕

1888年京都市下京区に生まれる。1903年京都府立第2中学中退後、洋画を学びはじめ、聖護院洋画研究所に入所、浅井忠の教えを受ける。1908年渡仏、アカデミー・ジュリアン等に学び、ルノワールに師事。女性像、風景画を主に描く。1913年帰国、翌年二科会創立に参加。留学の成果を日本的な油彩画へ展開させた。1920年兜屋畫堂で個展。1920～1921再び渡仏。1922年春陽会創立に参加。1925年国画創作協会洋画部創設に参加。1928年国画会創設に参加。同年野島康三邸にてデッサン展。浮世絵、桃山絵画の影響を取り入れた豪華で力強い画風を確立。女性像のほか、桜島、北京の風景をそれぞれ連作で描く。1934年頃から、岩絵の具を油で溶いて用い始めた。戦後は富士、浅間山をよく描き、薔薇を好んで描いた。1986年東京で死去。主著に『天衣無縫』がある。

萬鐵五郎〔TETSUGORO YOROZU〕

1885年岩手県和賀郡東和町土沢に生まれる。幼時より絵のてほどきをうけ、日本画を独習。早稲田中学に在学中より禅宗を学ぶ。1905年から白馬会第2研究所に通う。中学卒業後に禅宗布教のため渡米（約1年）し、帰国後の1907年から東京美術学校西洋画予備科に入学。1911年広島晃甫らとアブサント会を結成。1912年の卒業制作はフォーヴィスムを独自に研究した「裸体美人」であった。同年のヒュウザン会結成に参加。院展、二科展、日本版画創作協会展などに出品。キュービスムを解釈した静物、風景、人物像を制作。1919年二科会会友。このころより江戸期文人画を研究、さらに南画に傾倒した。1922年春陽会の設立に客員として参加。1922年野島康三邸で初めての日本画展。同年、小林徳三郎らと円鳥会を結成。1927年茅ケ崎にて死去。木版画にもすぐれ、評論も書いた。『鉄人独語』などの著書もある。

兜屋畫堂活動歴

大正 8 年（1919）
■3月29日──兜屋披露宴／於上野精養軒
斎藤與里、織田一磨、石井柏亭、梅原龍三郎、
正宗得三郎、津田青楓、山本鼎、長原孝太郎、
岡田三郎助、藤島武二らを招待
■5月3日～4日──開堂招待／趣意書発行
国内同時代の作家による洋画、彫刻、美術工芸
（中原悌二郎、富本憲吉も参加）
■6月1日～25日──新進洋画家新作展
硲伊之助、関根正二、鍋井克之、保田龍門、
林倭衛、山崎省三（6作家約20点）
■8月1日～25日──兜屋畫堂第一回素描展覧会

織田一磨	「虎の門外」
川上涼花	「夕の樹々」「風の日」「丘の冬」等計10点
森田恒友	「利根川の堤」
坂本繁二郎	「老母」「馬」「山羊」
中原悌二郎	「男の顔」
石井鶴三	「夜相撲」「夜相撲」「弁当」
斎藤與里	「ダンス」「水浴」「少女の顔」
梅原龍三郎	2点
山崎省三	「女」
鍋井克之	「種牛」
保田龍門	「前向きの女」計2点
栗原亮	「顔」
清水保雄	「寝顔」（13作家 30点）

■9月3日～25日──関根正二遺作展覧会
（1913～19年の油彩、素描計77点）
●1913 「荷上げ」「夏木立ち」「小名木川」「静」
●1915 「キリスト昇天」「十字架」「牛」「無題」
「習作」「男」「夕べ」「木のぼりする子供等」「農婦」
●1916 「習作」「海」「土蔵」「秋」「風景」「近郊」
「小牛」「河岸」（一）（二）（三）「労働者の群」「近
郊」「無題」「木のある河岸」
●1917 「A氏の像」「自畫像」「長野近郊」「裏
の娘」「河岸」（四）「少女」「椿」（屏風）
●1918 「静物」「少女」「市川」「小供」「小供」
「小供」「少女」「婦人」「馳出す女」「チュウリップ」
「信仰の悲しみ」「姉弟」「春の日のなやみ」「自畫
像」「那須温泉」「無題」「飛んで行く女」「少女」
「寝顔」「女」「圓光」の下畫「果實を運ぶ女」
●1919年 「三星」「小供」「梅ゆる前」「アネモ
ネ」「小岩驛附近」「小供」「春」「無題」「自畫像」
「小供」「少女」「小供の顔」「生」「死（慰められつ
つ悩むの続き）」「手」「畫稿」「手」「無題」「畫稿」
「恐怖」「青春」
●展覧会カタログ「信仰の悲しみ」発行
「関根正二氏遺作展覧会に際して」斎藤與里「関
根君と霊感『其他』」三瀦末松「関根君の事ども」
村岡黒影「関根君」佐々木猛「関根正二兄の死
を悼む」赤司尚道「思ひ出づるままに」太田三郎
「関根根のこと」津田青楓
■9月28日～10月6日（29日、16日?）──兜屋
主催洋画展覧会
審査員 安井曾太郎、梅原龍三郎、斎藤與里
募集作100余点から審査により22点を入選、展示
前田寛治らが入選
■10月1日～19日（8日～19日?）──織田一磨
個人展覧会（自画石版 45点）

●1919 「大阪風景（20点一組）」「日野春の雪
景山」「河岸の荷場」「宇治風景（水力発電所）」
「三勝半七、文楽座舞台」「小料理店（4点一
組）」「津村別院」「住吉」など
■10月21日～11月9日──装飾美術家協会作品展覧
原三郎、西村敏彦、岡田三郎助、渡辺素舟、
高村豊周、長原孝太郎、藤井達吉、今和三郎、
斎藤圭三、廣川松五郎（10作家31点）
■11月11日～30日──村山槐多遺作展／14日
に追悼会（1914～19年の油彩34点、水彩7点、
素描40数点）
●1914 「少女」「小杉氏庭園にて」「田端にて」
「二人の少年」「日光にて」「植物園」「房州船形に
て」「紙風船をかむれる自畫像」「少年の顔A」
「少年の顔B」
●1915 「無題」「Nの肖像」「尿する裸僧」「裸
の自像」「信州風景（1）～（5）」「女」「少女」
●1916 「カンナと少女」「大島の水汲女」「大島
風景」「村のポンプ庫」「自畫像（大島にて）」「目
黒附近」「自畫像」「娘」「無題」
●1917 「女の兄の顔」「湖水と女」「四谷荒木町
の一部」「乞食と女」「樹木」「デッサン」「クロッキ
（1）～（7）」
●1918 「男の習作」「煙草をのむ男」「立てる
女」「松と家」「松と榎」「松の群A」「松の群B」
「雪の次の日」「未央生の休息」「自畫像」「峠に
て」「山地の風景」「自畫像」「デッサン」「風船を
つく女A」「風船をつく女B」
●1919 「木のある風景」「佐々木の風景」「某侯
爵邸遠望」「佐々木の一部」その他番外素描十数点
●展覧会カタログを発行
「槐多君の遺作展に際して」（山崎省三）、「追想」
（長島重）、「京都に於ける村山の印象」（山本路
郎）、「第二の恋人」（白石源一郎）、「槐多君の
ために」（小柳正）、「略伝を記した後に」（今関啓
司）、「槐多君」（山本鼎）、「村山槐多君の遺作
展覧会」（斎藤與里）、「村山槐多略伝」（山崎・
今関共編）
■12月18日～25日──ロダン氏デッサン複製展覧会

大正 9 年（1920）
■1月9日～10日──ロダン素描複製展覧会
■1月15日～30日──日本版画協会第2回展覧会
中止
■1月20日～31日──石井鶴三第1期制作発表会
彫刻
●1916 「女」「中原氏像」「男」
●1917 「習作」
●1918 「首」「習作」
●1919 「足」
水彩、素描
●1912 「森の老爺と少女」「夢」「農婦」
●1913 「曲馬」「渓谷」「那須野」「山村の小学校」
●1914 「相撲」「夕」「夢」
●1915 「小学校」「朝」「朴の若葉」「鑿」「自画
像」「兎」「山の鳥」「温泉」「どろぼう」「猫」「夢」
「縊死者」
●1916 「自画像」「猫」「朴の若葉」「行旅病者」
「井戸を掘る」「自画像」「峠」「月」「幼虫」「夢」
「山茶花」「村相撲」
●1917 「競走」「蛙の産卵」「肖像」「山茶花」

fig.16:関根正二遺作展画集／兜屋畫堂発行／1919／
資料7

（1，2）「自画像」
●1918 「きやり」「自画像」「雷鳥」「山の鳥」「温
泉」「夜汽車」「嬰児」「山茶花」「夏の山」「自画
像」「赤牛」「紅葉と女」
●1919 「泣く子」「新緑」「感電」「冬」（1，2）
「秋」（1，2，3）「村娘」「習作」「山のスケッチ」
「踊り子」「夜相撲」（1，2，3）「春の水」「花見
のあと」
■2月18日～29日（19日?～）──児童自由画展
覧会
山本鼎、石井鶴三、長原孝太郎選
石井鶴三の妹と長野県の子供の作品
●展覧会カタログ発行（山本鼎執筆）
■3月2日～15日──鍋井克之個人展覧会
（1914～20年の18点）
●1920 「枯草の中の橋」「蕾をふくむ頃」「田園
小景初夏」「田園小景早春」「初夏の田含路」「風
景」
●1919 「新緑の路」「小川の風景」「初夏の路」
「雨の大根畑」「雪の路」「六月の田園」「海」
●1918 「池畔の早春」「秋」
●1915 「日を受けた森」
●1914 「市内スケッチ」（他1点）
●展覧会カタログ発行
■3月16日～31日──林倭衛個人展覧会
（1916～20年の作品10数点）
●1916 「多摩川附近」
●1917 「小笠原風景」「冬の海」
●1918 「海に沿ふてゆく道」「H氏肖像」
●1919 「少女」「梅雨期」「廣瀬氏肖像」「川べ
りの道」
●年代不詳「白い倉と海」「冬」「上高地深林」「冬
のうすれ日」
●展覧会カタログ発行
■4月1日～15日──中川一政個人展覧会
（1914～20年の作品31点）
●1914 「酒蔵」「監獄の横」
●1915 「霜のとける道」「少女肖像」「春光」「椅
子の少女」「薄日さす芋畑」

fig.17:中原悌二郎作／憩へる女(1919)／野島康三撮影

- 1916 「監獄裏の茶畑1」「杉と茶畑のある風景」
- 1917 「けぶれる冬」「監獄の横2」「監獄の横3」「夕日落つる踏切」「鵠沼の或る道」「野娘（エチュード）」「少女素描淡彩」「初冬」
- 1918 「監獄裏の茶畑2」
- 1919 「肖像断片」「冬の路傍」「下坂橋の川辺」「暮春の景色」「初夏水辺」「監獄裏の日没」「池袋の麦畑」「下坂橋の景色」「監獄の横4」
- 1920 「監獄の横5」「静物1」〜「静物3」
- 展覧会カタログ発行
■4月17日〜30日——碌伊之助個人展覧会 中止
■5月2日〜10日——恩地孝四郎個人展覧会
(1915〜19年の絵画26点、水彩1点、素描22点、画稿3点、土偶6点、計57点)
「静物」(4)、(5)、(8)、「春」「人物」(1)〜(4)「二性相闘」「愛の進行」素描(33)〜(36)「アマリリスの出芽」「解剖像」「台に林檎」「黒布と林檎」「静かに思ふ時」「アマリリス出芽」など
- 展覧会カタログ発行
■5月13日〜23日(〜30日?)——大森商二素描展
(1916年3点、1917年53点　計56点)
「雨後街道」「中野早春」「村落と墓地」「麦秋」「卓上静物」など
■5月25日〜30日——梅原龍三郎個人展覧会
■5月26日〜30日——山崎省三個人展覧会
(1916〜20年の素描と油彩)
- 1916 「午後の火薬庫」
- 1917 「自画像」
- 1918 「裸体習作A」「裸体習作B」
- 1919 「座せる御宿の女」「裸体」
- 1920 「少女の顔」ほか
- 不明 「トロクに乗る三人の子供」「切り通し風景」「信州にて」
■6月2日〜5日——小山敬三個人展覧会
(1911〜20年の作品39点)
- 1911 「草萌えの頃」
- 1916 「風の日の午後（朝鮮）」
- 1918 「砂丘の冬」「子牛等遊ぶ大島の海岸」「卓上草花図」「テニスを遊ぶ人々」「青年の肖像」
- 1919 「馬鈴薯と金柑と」「南湖院風景」「多摩川べり」
- 1920 「安房の草山」「草山」(1, 2)「自画像」「奈良風景」「奈良の春光」「いちいの森」「陽光に映ゆる山」ほか
■6月吉日——閉堂

野島康三邸展覧会活動歴

大正10年（1921）
■12月17日〜19日——富本憲吉氏作品展覧会
(1922年の作品)

大正11年（1922）
■5月25日〜29日——岸田劉生個人展覧会*
● 油彩・テンペラ
「麗子洋装座像」「童女立像」「童女飾髪圖」「椿花圖」「窓外早春」「野童女」「笑童女」「麗子」「村嬢圖」
● 水彩・素描
「麗子洋装」「河野君肖像」「麗子微笑」「麗子肖像」「村嬢図」「麗子肖像」「麗子微笑」「笑ふ麗子」
● 半切畫
「野童圖」「五福祥集」「童女圖」「裸童圖」「寒山拾得」「童女食菓圖」「両拳圖」「童女遊戯圖」(近作25点)
■7月8日〜10日——萬鐵五郎日本画展*
「砂丘の冬」「夕立つ濱」「六月の畫」「若葉の頃」「村の道」「芋苗の育つ頃」「小径農舎」「T字路」「松風濱荘」「水と舟」「砂丘の家」「郊外の初夏」「水に戯れる人達」「桑柴行人」「早春」「對話」「木の芽出し」「麦の秋」(18点)
■10月21日〜23日——横堀角次郎油絵個人展覧会*
「自畫像」「代々木の町はずれ」「上山崎の崖」「土と草」「崖下の道」「海之行く道」「風の吹く日」「S君の肖像」「太郎右衛門淵遠望」「赤土の山より大崎の一部を望む」「崖上の道」「水たまり」「静物」「切り開かれた地」「上水台とそのほとり」「真夏の赤土坂道」「赤土の山」「切通し坂」「秋」「冬」「赤土の山」「初夏」「日のあたっている小坂道」「静物」「別荘地の路」「鵠沼小景」「川べり」「静物」(1915〜1922までの28点)
■12月2日〜4日——小林徳三郎個人展覧会*
● 1909 「顔」● 1910 「品川風景」● 1911 「新大橋」● 1913 「母と子」● 1914 「畫家の家族」● 1915 「風景」● 1916 「某夫人肖像」● 1918 「鴛鴦」(衝立装飾)● 1919「鰯」(其の一)● 1921「鰯」(其の二)● 1922「丘の一部」「ステッキを持つ子」「いけだ橋」「鐵橋」　(15点)
■12月21日〜23日——富本憲吉氏作品展
(陶器百数十点)

大正13年
■5月17日〜19日——富本憲吉氏陶器展
(近作百数十点)

大正14年（1925）
■5月——富本憲吉展

昭和3年（1928）
■10月26日〜28日——梅原龍三郎デッサン展
「裸婦像」「裸婦結髪」(一)〜(三)、「裸婦鏡」「裸婦花籠」「裸婦白衣」「浴婦」「臥裸婦」「裸婦」「静浦月」(一)〜(三)、「静浦朝」「静浦雨後」「立つ裸婦」「チュリップ」「カンヌ港」ほか (近作彩色デッサン30余点出品)

昭和7年（1932）
■時期不明——朝鮮李朝陶器展覧会

〈凡例〉
● 展覧会、出品作品とも、現在確認できるもののみを記した。表は野島康三の行った全展覧会ではない。ことに野島邸での展覧会については現在確認できる記録が少なく、今後の調査に期待したい。
● 展覧会に際して出版されたカタログ類で、筆者が確認できたものは内容の目次を付し、出版が確認できたものには、その旨のみを記した。
● 展覧会に際して作成された出品記録を、筆者が確認した場合には展覧会名末尾に*印を付した。
● 会期については文献によって異なるため、原則的に会期終了後の文献に従ったが、判断できない場合は2種類の会期を記したものがある。

野島康三美術作品撮影・出版活動

1921年（大正10年）
中原悌二郎作品集／図版撮影野島康三／日本美術院出版（平櫛田中編集）
1924年（大正13年）〜1927年（昭和2年）
富本憲吉模様集(全3巻、コロタイプ印刷)／野島康三撮影、限定20部／自家出版
1932年（昭和7年）〜1933年（昭和8年）
雑誌『光画』／（第1巻1号〜第2巻12号、全18冊）聚楽社発行（第1巻1号〜6号）、光画社発行（第2巻1号〜12号）
1933年（昭和8年）
富本憲吉陶器集／野島康三監修、限定20部／自家出版／錦古里孝治撮影
1937年（昭和12年）
「梅原龍三郎画集」　春鳥会出版、限定100部所収／「アトリエの1日」写真10葉　野島康三撮影

野島康三文書

［差出人名］	［日付］	［数量］	［備考］
石井柏亭	1933〜1934	2	
石井鶴三	1922〜1931	3	
川島理一郎	1934〜1935	2	
木村荘八	?〜1924〜?	3	大正期か?
岸田劉生	1922	9	
小林徳三郎	1924〜1941?	4	
中川一政	1920?〜1929?	64	
斎藤與里	1921	4	
椿貞雄	1933〜1937	3	
梅原龍三郎	1921〜1941?	60	
萬鐵五郎	1921〜1922	19	
富本憲吉	1921〜1927?	145	
浜田庄司	?	1	1920年代か?
柳宗悦	1922〜1935?	37	
有島武郎	?	2	大正期頃
田中喜作	1921〜1934?	20	
長與善郎	1932	1	
阿部能成	?〜1934〜1942	4	
野上豊一郎	1924〜1944〜?	43	
野上弥生子	?		昭和初期

（飯沢耕太郎／光田由里／ジェフリー・ギルバート編）

野島康三のことば

■「朱雪雑記」（写真月報 第25巻 第3号）より
1920（大正9）年

寫眞に自分の心（私の心を透してみた自然……
結極は私の人格の表現……）を生すにはどうする
のか……
私は美術寫眞とか藝術寫眞とか云ふ言葉をやた
らに用ひますまい……この言葉を安價に解釈して、
そして安價なものを作つておられないのですから。
私の心から生れ出たものは私自身では唯の普通
の寫眞のつもりでゐても私の心を見てくれる人々に
は私の尊い心がそれに生きてゐることを見てくれま
す。
私はそういうものが作りたいのです。
自然のゆつたりした氣持ちになつて普通の寫眞を
作りたいのです。
繪のやうな寫眞だなど云はれて嬉しがつてゐて
は駄目です。
寫眞には寫眞の世界があります。
寫眞の世界に作家が生きていなければ駄目で
す。

頭も作りたい。
腕も作りたい。
一番だいじな心を大切に育てたい。
ともかく勉強することです。

私は私の進むべき道をどこまでも歩るいてゆきま
す。
一生の仕事です。　　　（1920・2・7）

■「朱雪雑記」（写真月報 第25巻 第4号）より
1920（大正9）年

自己の心に生きた寫眞を作ることを、ほんとに自分
の仕事だと信ずる、根底のある作家が出なくてはこ
まります。
毎年展覧会を見てゐて、ちつともさういふ、しつか
りした氣持ちのするものに出逢はないのは實に淋し
い氣持がします。
　　自然に感激する
　　其自然を寫す
　　自然の型が出來る
　　そこには自然より受けた感激は消えて
　　感激を授けた自然の型が出來る
　　これが一般の寫眞です
寫眞は簡単に出來易いものです。
仕事をするにしても、わずかの時間を総合せて作
れるものです。それですから、どれも幾日も其の仕
事の爲めに時間を用意して充分に心をおちつけて
作ることをやらないやうです。
これではとても、よいものは出來ますまい。

もつと、もつと本氣になつて作つて下さい。そして作
る時の氣持ちや、寫眞の仕事を尊重していゝ加減
な態度でなく本氣になつて作つて下さい。きつと
いゝものが生れます。
私は作る時には、どうしても充分の時間が欲しいの

です。一日心を其仕事に投入することが出來なけ
れば駄目です。
　　頭脳と技巧が心によつて生かされた時によい
　　作品が生まれる。
　　頭脳の人、技巧の人にはなりたくない
　　心の人になりたい
　　そして其心を生かす頭脳と技巧とが欲しいも
　　のです。

■「朱雪雑記」（写真月報 第25巻 第5号）より
1920（大正9）年

よく、力があつていゝと稱する黒つぽい色をした、強
い感じのもの（オイルやゴム）には、どうもきたない、
やりつぱなしのものがよくあつて困ります。これは其
の材料のあつかい方の悪いせいです。材料の扱
ひ方をのみ込んで、おちついて作れば強い感じで
氣持いゝもの出來ます。
つまり技術の未熟なところへ、あわてゝ、いゝ加減
なものを作るからいけないのです。
作品の持つ力は作者の心の深い淺いによつて、き
まります。こゝに心をもるだけのよき頭、よき腕のとも
なう事はきまつたことです。
　　此のよきと云ふ意味は俗にいふ下手上手のこ
　　とではありません。作者の心をもるために生れ
　　た作者自身だけが所有するところの獨特なも
　　のゝことです。
カビネ大のものでも随分いゝものが作れます。手札
でも、いゝもの作れることがあります。
半切大の空虚な、たるみきつた作品を見ると、憐れ
な氣持ちがします。
　　藝術は量よりも質の問題です。
林檎も梨も寫せば丸い黒つぽいものに寫る。
そして、きたない感じにみへる場合が多い。
ほんとのものは、林檎と梨とはまるで感じがちがふ。
一つは艶のある美しい色をもつもの、一つは艶のな
い澁い色をしたおちつきのあるもの。
それが只の黒いかたまりではこまる。
黒く寫つても差支へないから、その黒さに、ほんも
のゝ美しさを表現すればいい。
只の黒のかたまりでなく林檎或は梨の美しさをつ
かんだ美しい黒でありたい。
蜜柑も黒く寫る。
しかし林檎とくらぶれば形と面が違ふからすぐにわ
かる。それは、形の變化であつて蜜柑の美しさ林
檎の美しさのちがひではない。
蜜柑のみづみづしい、やわらかい感じがほしい。

■「孤雲録（三）」（日本写真会会報第2巻第5
号）より　1927（昭和2）年

構圖断片

こゝに與へられたる（寫さんとして用意したる）材料
を、どういふ風に置いたら生かされるか。どういふ風
な見方をしたら生かすことが出來るかと、智慧をは
たらかしてその材料をいろいろに配置してみる。
つまり組立をしてみる。
それを與へられたる、（或は撰び出したる）紙面の
上に、例へば八ツ切、四ツ切、等におさむるには
如何にすべきかと思案をする。
それによつて己れの氣のすむやう、これなら寫して

もいゝと安心のゆくやうに案配する。つまり構圖する
ことである。

そこで大切なことは、その材料を生かすことである。
いゝ工合に組立が出來て、そこに統一があり、安定
があり、明暗の調子が調つておれば、それは自然
と構圖上の法則にあてはまるものである。

首めからその法則などによつて自然を見、又靜物
の材料などを見ないで「美」をめがけて仕事する方
がいゝと思ふ。
もつとも「美」をつかむ順序として一通りは法則の心
得がある方がいゝといふかもしれないが、それは第
二義、第三義の問題であつて己れの観察によつ
てつかんでゆく方がいゝと思ふ。そのかたはら先人
の作品を研究し、それを滋養分としてとり入れた方
がいゝと思ふ。

とにかくある寸法の紙面のなかに、おさめこむことが
構圖するといふ事になる。
一幅の畫を作るためには構圖がどうしても必要だと
いふことになる。

構圖ばかりよくてもいゝ作品とはいへぬ。
いゝ作品はきつと構圖がいゝものだ。

勉強

秀でたる才能なくとも勉強によつて手堅いものを作
る境地には達せらるゝものだ。
よき作品を熱心に見ることはいゝことだ。
いろいろ異なつた作風のものを多く見るよりは己れ
の氣に入つた作品を熱心に見る方がいゝと思ふ。
そうして自然の見方に見當をつける。
それゆえ或る人の作風に傾倒しすぎると、作つたも
のがその人の作風を模倣してゐるように見られるこ
とがある。
又作者自身も明かに模倣を感じて作ることがある
だらう。
これも勉強する一つの方法であつて、その場合に
はその態度を徹底させる方がいゝと思つてゐる。そう
して自然を深く見、味ふことがわかつてくると、いつ
のまにかその作者の作風が生れてくるものだ。（但
し作風を生む作者はかなりえらい人で、なかなか出
ない）。
ともかく、見ること、作ること。

■人物作畫法（アルス寫眞大講座）より
1929（昭和4）年

私は背像をつくるとき、その對象を適當な光を受くる
位置においてまづながめる。
さうして明暗、形を調べる。
面白いなと思つたらすぐに寫す。
私はそのときにその人物の性格を寫し出さうとか、
殊更に特長をめつけ出して寫さうとか思はない。
明暗、形からくる感覺によつて寫す。
そこに面白味を見出すのである。
又表情にひかれて寫すときもあるが、主として問題
になるのはやはり明暗、形である。
　　　　　　　　□
表情を主として、その表面より生まれる一種の氣分

を寫し出さうとする方法もあるであらうが私には出來ない。

私は造形の面白味の方により多く興味を感じる。とにかく感覺を主として仕事しなくてはいけないと思ふ。

□

感覺を主とするといつても妙に歪めたのや、むやみにボヤボヤしてゐる作品、畫画の亂雜なものは好まない。

奇をてらひ、變態の感じをねらふなどはいやなことである。

清新、健康、溫雅なものでありたい。

□

私が對象物を寫さうと思つたときは、そのものの持つ（表現してゐる）ときである。そのとき私は、私をひきつけてゐる美しさが何處にひそんでゐるかを充分にしらべる。さうして與へられてゐる美をめがけて寫せばいいのだ。

□

自然の姿、生々したところをつかむことが重要である。

明暗、形は自然の姿をよりよく生かす方法である。

それが反對に明暗、形のみ調つて自然さを失つては對象が生きてこない。

明暗、形の美によつて對象を充分に生かした仕事をしたい。

■「思ふこと」（光画第1巻第1号）より　1932（昭和7）年

○

藝術は感覺を生命としてゐると思ふ。

感覺が清新でなければ「美」は發見出來ない。

概念で物を見たり、作つたりしてゐては生命あるものはわからない、出來もしない。

感覺の魅力に生きたものが作りたい。

○

平凡にみへて、やつてみると平凡にあらざるものがある。

そこに仕事の深さがあると思ふ。

■「雑記」（光画第1巻第5号）より　1932（昭和7）年

私はどうも人間を寫すのが好きだ。殊に顔に興味がある。

同じモデルの顔を毎日寫してゐてもあきないのだ。

モデルも其日其日によつて氣持ちや身體の工合などで表情や皮膚の感じが異つてゐる。私の方も同じやうに其日其日によつて見方が異つてくる。

とにかく良いものが出來る出來ないにかかわらず寫す時はつづけさまに澤山寫しておく。何か寫したい慾望を感じて寫してゐる間が實にいいものだ。

現像をして氣に入つた板が出來ると新たな喜びが生れる。

三人ぐらいのモデルを交替に毎日寫せたらさぞ面白いことであらうと思つてゐる。

このやうな事は未だ試みてみないので、どんなものかわからないが、出來たら樂しみ深いことだらうと思ふ。

モデルが來てくれるときまつた仕事が出來てい。

仕事場で氣持よく仕事の出來ることは此の上もな

い喜びだ。

■「思ふこと」（光画第1巻第6号）より　1932（昭和7）年

○

ぬけがらのやうな人物寫眞が多い。

○

寫眞によつて生かされた人間の寫つてゐるものは稀れだ。

○

私はこの生かされた魅力ある人間が作りたいと思つてゐる。

■「雑記」（光画第2巻第1号）より　1933（昭和8）年

寫眞界も新興寫眞なるもの、出現によつて一時にどぎまぎしたやうであつたが、これはかなりいい藥であつた。この藥は是非必要なものであつたのだ。この藥もすつかり行きわたつたやうだし、それを吸收して取るべきを取り、捨つべきを捨てやゝおちつきを見せてゐるやうだ。

しかし此の仕事はもつとつつ込んで行かなければいけない事だから、いい加減な早のみこみで理解したやうな顔をしてしまつてはいけないと思ふ。寫眞が良くなり面白くなるのはこれからだと思ふ。寫眞に對する理解も深められつつあることだし、表現型式の自由さがづつと擴げられてゐるから新進の人々に期待するところが多い。

光畫も其意味に於て何等かの役目をはたしたいと希つてゐる。自分達でやらなければいけないと思ふ仕事を持つ事が必要だ。

今年は光畫のために大いに努力したいと思ふ。

■「藝術寫眞から見た報導寫眞―寫眞に於ける智情意」（アサヒカメラ5月号）より　1941（昭和16）年

A:世間ではこの時代に藝術寫眞など作つてゐるのは怪しからん、もつと世の中に有用な仕事をしろといふ聲も聞えてきますよ。

B:さうですか。それはほんきでいつてゐるのでせうか。役に立つといふこと、これは文字や言葉では無造作にいへますが、ほんとうはなかなか大きな意味が含まれてゐると思ふのです。目先だけ役に立つことにも言へるでせう。じわじわしみ渡つて大きな力を與へるために役に立つことにもいへるでせう。ところで世間では目先だけに役に立ちさへすればいいと考へる方が多いのぢやありませんか。

A:いやに君はおちついてゐるが、寫眞の力で社會を國家が望んでゐる方向へ進むのに役に立つ仕事をやつてもらへたらと思ふのですが、出來ませんか。

B:だしぬけに今度は大きく出てきましたね。私は藝術寫眞も必要、科學寫眞も必要、報道寫眞も必要だと思つてゐます。智情意といふ文字がありますが、科學寫眞は智、藝術寫眞は情、意は報道寫眞にあてはめてもいいと思ふのです。人間に智情意が備はつてゐなければ動物と同じことで、人間のありがたみはなくなつてしまひます。寫眞の世界もやうやく人間並に世の中に獨立した一つの立派な

仕事をなしとげる物として存在する價値が出來たのぢやありませんか。

A:藝術寫眞だけが寫眞だと思ひ、報道寫眞だけを寫眞だけ思つてゐてはこまりますね。

B:寫眞をやる人の才能にまかせて、苦勞出來る方向の仕事をやつたらいゝぢやありませんか。私は藝術寫眞をやります。君は報道寫眞がやりたかつたらやつたらいゝでせう。苦勞して、そこに喜びを求めることの出來る仕事をすることですよ。

A:いろいろお說教をきかされてしまつたが。ところで、君は今の報道寫眞について意見はありませんか。

B:科學寫眞では寫眞の持つ現實性、記錄性を生かして、そこに食ひこんで仕事をすればいいのですが、報道寫眞ではその特性を基礎にしてそこの情景を傳へる内容の力が大きな役割を持つと思ひます。ある時は意志表示の役割をもつとめなければならないでせう。

A:そこで國家の指令に從つて報道寫眞家は動員されて働くといふこともあり得るわけですね。君のいふやうに苦勞して仕事するには、それだけの腕がなければ出來ないことです。腕は頭がにぶくては苦勞しようつたつて苦勞する種がないわけですからね。

B:藝術寫眞家には感覺の確かな人がたくさんゐますが報道寫眞家には乏しいやうに思ひます。これからきつと才能のある優れた報道寫眞家が出て來るのぢやないかと思つてゐるのです。

（光田由里編）

備考:旧漢字、かな使いは、できる限り初出のまま再録し、誤字、脱字等も訂正せず、原文のまま再録した。

主要参考文献抄

単行本

■野島康三遺作集：野島康三遺作集刊行会／1965年／日本フォトセンター株式会社
〈所収〉「野島康三君の想い出」梅原龍三郎／「野島康三さんのこと」木村伊兵衛／「野島さんのこと」伊奈信男／「〈女の顔〉展のころ」原弘／「ピリリともゆるがない信念」ハナヤ勘兵衛／「野島さんの思い出」島田巽／「思い出すまま」吉川富三／「感謝とお詫び」北角玄三／「野島さん追想」錦古里孝治／「野々宮の思い出」堀不佐夫／「野島さん御夫妻と三十年」掛下尚吉／「K・C・C時代を顧みて」山口節三／「野島先生と日本フォトセンター」大谷隆三／「野島先生の微笑」芳賀日出男／「野島先生」船山克／「野島先生とNIKONグループ」大場栄一／「遺作集刊行にあたって」藤井利雄
■ Modern Photography 1934-35, Studio Annual, by Geffrey Holme, London, 1935
■現代日本名作写真画集：写真新報社／1935年
世界写真全集・別巻―歴史的展望：伊奈信男ほか共著／1959年／平凡社
■写真130年史：田中雅夫／ダヴッド社／1959年
国画会・写真三十年：国画会・写真三十年編集委員会編／1969年
〈所収〉「野島康三大人」ハナヤ勘兵衛／「回想」錦古里孝治／「野島さんと私」吉川富三
■日本写真史1840-1945：日本写真家協会／1971年／平凡社
〈所収〉「芸術写真」多木浩二
■カメラ・アイ一転形期の現代写真：重森弘淹／1974年／日貿出版社
〈所収〉「1930年代のまなざし―安井仲治と野島康三」
■対談・写真この50年：木村伊兵衛／アサヒカメラ編／朝日新聞社／1975年
〈所収〉「懐かしきベス単のころ」
■日本写真史年表：日本写真協会編／1976年／講談社
■写真・昭和50年史：伊奈信男／1978年／朝日新聞社
〈所収〉「日本近代写真の夜明け―光画と野島康三」
■現代日本写真全集日本の美第4巻―京いろとかたち：1978年／集英社
〈所収〉「福原信三と野島康三―芸術写真の推進者」重森弘淹
■大正感情史：飯沢耕太郎ほか共著／1979年／日本書籍
〈所収〉「大正の質感」飯沢耕太郎
■ A Century of Japanese Photography introduction by John Dower, Japan Photographers Association, 1980, Pantheon Books, Random House, New York
■日本の裸像：1981年／朝日ソノラマ
悲喜劇　1930年代の建築と文化：同時代建築研究会編／1982年／現代企画室
〈所収〉「『光画』を読む」伊藤俊治
■ International Center for Photography Encyclopedia of Photography, 1st ed. Crown Pub., New York, 1984
■芸術写真とその時代：飯沢耕太郎／1986年／筑摩書房
〈所収〉「凝視する精神―野島康三論」
■日本写真全集第2巻―芸術写真の系譜：1986年／小学館
〈所収〉「写真と絵画（二）」澤本徳美／"The Heritage of Art Photograhpy in Japan", by Jeffery Gilbert
■日本写真全集第3巻―近代写真の群像
〈所収〉「『光画』と現実写真」飯沢耕太郎／"The Modern Photography Movement in Japan" by Jeffery Gilbert
■日本写真全集第5巻―人物と肖像：1986年／小学館
〈所収〉「人物作画　野島熙正」（再録）
■日本写真全集第6巻―ヌードフォト：1986年／小学館
〈所収〉「野島康三の足跡」重森弘淹
■日本近代写真の成立　関東大震災から真珠湾まで：金子隆一、柏木博、伊藤俊治、長谷川明／1987年／青弓社
〈所収〉「日本ピクトリアリズム写真とその周辺」金子隆一／「野島康三と『光画』」伊藤俊治
■ヌード写真の見方：飯沢耕太郎／1987年／新潮社
■光画の時代―写真に帰れ：飯沢耕太郎／1988年／平凡社
■カメラ面白物語：1988年／朝日新聞社
■都市の視線―日本の写真1920-30年代：飯沢耕太郎／1989年／創元社
〈所収〉「野島康三―日本近代写真の確立者」
■東京身体映像：伊藤俊治／1990年／平凡社
〈所収〉「"都市の女たち"の発見―『光画』時代の野島康三」「『光画』を読む―写真の1930年代」
■光画全3巻：解題／飯沢耕太郎／1990年／復刻版『光画』刊行会
■劉生絵日記（第1巻）：岸田劉生著／1952年／龍生閣
■岸田劉生全集（第7～8巻）：岸田劉生著／1980年／岩波書店
■劉生日記（第2巻）：岸田劉生著／1984年／岩波書店
■鉄人画論：萬鐵五郎著／土方定一編／1968年／中央公論美術出版
■中川一政文集（第5巻）：中川一政著／1976年／筑摩書房
〈所収〉「私の遍歴」

定期刊行物

■光画：第1巻第1号～第1巻第6号、聚楽社、1932年／第2巻第1号～第2巻第12号、光画社、1933年
■芦屋サロン：芦屋カメラクラブ／1935年～1940年
■写真月報：1920年4月号／「写真展覧会を観て」織田一磨／「野島氏の作品に就いて」山崎静村／「感想　野島君の作品を見て」川上涼花
■写真月報：1920年5月号／「第十回写真展覧会第三室」門外漠
■光画：1933年8月号／「写真展覧会の一つの形式として」原弘／「野島さんの近業」中川一政
■アサヒカメラ：1933年8月号／「写真月報／野島康三・女の顔展」板垣鷹穂
■写真月報：1933年8月号／「雑報／野島康三・女の顔展」
■フォトアート：1965年1月号／「ギャラリー点描／野島康三回顧展」
■アサヒカメラ：1965年1月号／「今月の広場／盛会だった「野島康三」回顧展」
■カメラ毎日：1965年7月号／「野島さんのこと」藤井利雄／「裸婦―野島康三遺作」
■カメラ毎日：1969年1月／「一品制作の重さ」大辻清司
■カメラ毎日：1972年3月号／「40年まえの前衛写真雑誌『光画』がめざしたもの」／「野島康三さんと"光画"の周辺」木村伊兵衛／「写真に帰れ（再録）」伊奈信男
■フォトアート：1972年3月号／「野島康三氏と雑誌「光画」をしのぶ会」
■アサヒカメラ：1972年6月／木村伊兵衛放談室6「昭和初めの社会派・耽美派」木村伊兵衛
■アサヒカメラ：1973年2月／木村伊兵衛放談室14「特集『写真開花期』の人と作品」木村伊兵衛
■アサヒカメラ：1972年4月増刊／「現代写真の源流をたずねて　特集2　野島康三と安井仲治」
■フォトアート：1974年9月／「破綻と彷徨―日本写真『近代』試論7　野島康三」福島辰夫
■アサヒカメラ：1975年3月／「写真・昭和五十年史5　日本近代写真の夜明け　『光画』と野島康三」伊奈信男
■ ICONICS：1982年3月／「野島康三と『光画』」飯沢耕太郎
■カメラ毎日：1983年4月／「日本近代写真の成立2　野島康三と光画」伊藤俊治
■アサヒカメラ：1985年7月／「写真史の視座から7　文化の成熟に向けて―スティーグリッツと野島康三」飯沢耕太郎
■北海道立近代美術館紀要：1986年3月／「『光画』について」地家光二
アサヒカメラ：1988年4月／「アンテイーク・イメージ館　近代写真の確立者野島康三」飯沢耕太郎
■視る（京都国立近代美術館）：1988年5月／「野島康三の芸術」ジェフェリー・ギルバート
■芸術新潮：1988年11月号／「写真て芸術！1930年代日本のモダン・フォトグラフ」飯沢耕太郎
■北海道旭川美術館紀要：1989年3月／「中原悌二郎と野島康三」越前俊也
■芸術新潮：1989年7月／「写真家が選んだ

昭和の写真ベスト10」
■ PACIFIC FRIEND：1989, vol. 17, no. 8／
「150 YEARS OF PHOTOGRAPHIC ART」
■太陽：1990年7月／「世界が創った肖像写真100枚」
■芸術新潮：1990年7月号／「大正が生んだ"写真文化人"野島康三」飯沢耕太郎

展覧会カタログ

■日本写真百年史展：日本写真家協会／1962年
■写真100年—日本人による写真表現の歴史：編集委員会編、日本写真家協会／1968年
■野島康三展／新宿ニコンサロン／1971年／三木潤テキスト
■現代日本写真史展：日本写真家協会編／1975年
■ Yasuzo Nojima, Fermi National Accelerator Laboratory Gallery, Illinois, 1979, introduction by Dr. Leon Lederman, essay by Jeffrey Gilbert
■写真と絵画展：東京都美術館／1978年
■シカゴ美術館所蔵写真展カタログ／1982年
■芸術としての写真・その誕生から今日まで—シカゴ美術館のコレクションから—：国立国際美術館／1984年
■つくば写真美術館'85　パリ・ニューヨーク・東京：つくば写真美術館／1985年
■ JAPON DES AVANT-GARDES 1910-1970／Musee national d'art moderne, Centre George Pompidou, 1986／"Nojima et l'avant-garde" par Jeffrey Gilbert／"La Photographie Japonaise ; Inventer Une Tradition" par Alain Sayag
■第60回記念展国画会写真部：国画会写真部／1986年
■日本の写真1930年代展：神奈川県立近代美術館／1988年
〈所収〉「新興写真の時代—東京を中心に—」飯沢耕太郎
■第63回50周年記念展国画会写真部：国画会写真部／1989年
■光画とその時代—1930年代の肖像写真：朝日新聞社／1989年
〈所収〉「『光画』という奇跡」飯沢耕太郎／「野島さんの名人芸—吉川富三氏に聞く」聞き手：飯沢耕太郎
■写真150年展—渡来から今日まで：写真150年展実行委員会／1989年
〈所収〉「『芸術写真』から『新興写真へ』」飯沢耕太郎
■ On the Art of Fixing a Shadow-150 Years of Photography／The National Gallery of Art, Washing ton D. C., The Art Institute of Chicago, 1989
■静物—言葉なきものたちの祭典：静岡県立近代美術館／1990年
■写真のモダニズム　国画会：国画会写真

部／1990年
■ La Photographie Japonaise de l'entre deux guerres, Du pictorialisme au modernisme, Mission du Patrimoine Photographique, 1990
"An Introduction to Nojima Yasuzo" by Jeffrey Gilbert

野島康三自筆文献

■「展覧会に第一部、第二部を設けるに就いて」／写真月報：第20巻第1号／1915年1月1日発行／写真月報社
■「朱雪雑記」（連載）／写真月報：第25巻第3号、1920年3月1日発行／第4号、4月1日発行／第5号、5月1日発行／第10号、10月1日発行／写真月報社
■「中原氏のこと」／『彫刻の生命』：中原悌二郎著　収録／1921年発行／アルス社
■「孤雲録」（連載）／日本写真会会報：第2巻第2号、1927年2月1日発行／第3号、3月1日発行／第4号、4月1日発行／第5号、5月1日発行／第3巻第1号、7月1日発行／日本写真会事務局
■「人物作画法」／アルス写真大講座第2巻／1929年発行／アルス社
■「思ふこと」（連載）／『光画』：第1巻第1号、1932年5月1日発行／第2号、6月10日発行／第3号、7月10日発行／第4号、9月10日発行／第5号、10月10日発行／第6号、11月24日発行／聚楽社
■「鉄道省制作映画『日本の四季』批判」／『光画』：第2巻第7号、1933年7月1日発行／光画社
■光画巻末雑記／『光画』：第1巻第1号、1932年5月1日発行／第2号、6月10日発行／第3号、7月10日発行／第4号、9月10日発行／第5号、10月10日発行／第6号、11月24日発行／聚楽社
第2巻第1号、1933年1月1日発行／第2号、2月1日発行／第3号、3月1日発行／光画社
■光画巻末雑録／『光画』：第2巻第8号，1933年8月20日発行／光画社
■「ワイキキの唄　布哇カメラ行脚」／アサヒカメラ：1936年7月号
■「芸術写真から見た報道写真—写真に於ける智情意」／アサヒカメラ：1941年6月号

（光田由里編）

SELECTED BIBLIOGRAPHY

Articles by Yasuzo Nojima

■ *Tenrankai ni daiichibu dainibu o mukeru ni tsuite* (*A Proposal to establish the unjuried section*), Shashin Geppo, Vol. 20, no. 1, 1915, Konishiroku

■ *Shusetsu zakki* (*Scarlet Snow Note*), Shashin geppo, Vol, 25, no. 3-5, 10, 1920, Shashin Geppo sha

■ *Nakahara shi no koto* (*Concerning Mr. Nakahara*), Chokoku no Seimei, by Tejiro Nakahara, 1921, Ars

■ *Kounroku* (*Traveling Cloud Note*), Nihon shashinkai kaiho, vol. 2, no. 2-5, vol. 3, no. 1, 1927, Nihon Shashinkai jimukyoku

■ *Jinbutsu Sakugaho* (*How to Make Pictures of People*), Ars Shashin Daikoza, 1929, Ars

■ *Omou koto* (*Some of my ideas*), Koga vol. 1, no. 1-6, 1932, Jurakusha

■ *Tetsudo sho seisaku eiga Nihon no shiki hihan* (*Critics of the cinema "Japanese seasons"*), Koga vol. 2, no. 7, 1933 Jurakusha

■ *Zakki* (*Note*), Koga, vol. 1, no. 1-6, 1932, Jurakusha, vol. 2, no. 1-3, 1933, Kogasha

■ *Zatsuroku* (*Records*), Koga vol. 2, no. 8, 1933, Kogasha

■ *Waikiki no uta Hawai camera angya* (*Traveling to Waikiki in Hawai with a Camera*), Asahi Camera, July, 1936

■ *Geijutu Shasin kara mita Hodo Shashin* (*An Art Photographer's point of view concerning News Photograhpy*), Asahi Camera, June, 1941

Books on Nojima

■ *Nojima Yasuzo Isakushu* (*Nojima Yasuzo Memorial Monograph*), Nojima Yasuzo Isaku Hozonkai, Tokyo, 1965

■ *Modern Photography 1934-35*, Studio Annual, by Geoffrey Holme, London, 1935

■ *Gendai Nihon Meisaku Shashin gashu* (*Selected Japanese contemporary photography*), Shashin shinpo sha, 1935

■ *Sekai shashin zensyu bekkan-rekisiteki tembo* (*World Photography, separate volume, History*), Heibonsha, 1959

■ *Shashin 130nen shi* (*History of Photography 130 years*), by Masao Tanaka, David sha, 1959

■ *Kokugakai shashin 30nenshi* (*History of Kokugakai Photography 30 years*), Kokugakai Shashin 30nenshi Henshuu Iinkai, 1969

■ *Nihon shashin shi 1840-1945* (*History of Japanese Photography*), Nihon Shashinka Kyokai, Heibonsha, 1971

■ *Camera eye-tenkeiki no gendai shashin* (*Camera eye-photography at the turning point*), by Koen Shigemori, Nichibo shuppansha, 1974

■ *Taidan-Shasin kono 50 nen* (*Conversations-50 years of photography*), Ihee Kimura, Asahi Shimbunsha, 1975

■ *Nihon shashin shi nempo* (*Chronology of Japanese photograhpy*), Nihon Shashin Kyokai, Kodansha, 1976

■ *Shashin Showa 50 nen shi* (*50 years of photography in Showa period*), Nobuo Ina, Asahi Shimbun sha, 1978

■ *Gendai Nihon shashin zenshu vol. 4, Nihon no bi* (*Japanese contemporary Photograhpy, vol. 4, Beauty of Japan*), Shueisha, 1978

■ *Taisho Kanjo si* (*A history of the feeling of the Taisho period*), Iizawa Kohtaro, Nihonshoseki, 1979

■ *A Century of Japanese Photography*, Japan Photographers Association, Pantheon Books, Random House, New York, 1980

■ *Nippon no Rafu* (*Japanese Nude*), Asahi Sonorama, 1981

■ *Hikigeki 1930 nendai no kentchku to bunka* (*Tragicomedy-Japanese Architecture and culture in 1930s*), Gendai Kikakushitsu, 1982

■ *International Center of Photography Encyclopedia of Photography*, 1st ed. Crown pub. New York, 1984

■ *Geijutsu Shashin to Sono Jidai* (*Art Photography in Japan 1900-1930*), by Kohtaro Iizawa, Chikuma Shobo, 1986

■ *Nihon shashin zenshu* (*The Complete History of Japanese Photography*) vol. 2, 3, 4, 5, 6, Shogakukan, 1986

■ *Nihon kindai shashin no seiritsu-Kanto Daishinsai kara Shinjuwan made* (*Establishment of Japanese Modern Photography-from the Great Kanto Earthquake to Pearl Harbor*), by Ryuichi Kaneko, Toshiharu Ito, Seikyusha, 1987

■ *Nude Shashin no mikata* (*How to Appreciate Nude photography*), Kohtaro Iizawa, Shinchosha, 1987

■ *Koga to sono jidai-Shashin ni Kaere* (*The time of Koga-Return to the Photography*), Kohtaro Iizawa, Heibonsha, 1988

■ *Camera Omoshiro monogatari* (*Episodes of Camera*), Asahi Shimbun sha, 1988

■ *Toshi no shizen-Nippon no shashin 1920-1930 nendai* (*Eyes of the City-Japanese Photography 1920s-1930s*), by Kohtaro Iizawa, Sogensha, 1989

■ *Tokyo shintai eizo* (*Images of Body in Tokyo*), by Toshiharu Ito, Heibonsha, 1990

■ *Koga fukkokuban zen 3 kan* (*Koga Reproduction, vol. 3*), Fukokuban Koga kanko kai, 1990

■ *Ryusei E nikki* (*Ryusei Kishida Diaries with his cuts*), by Ryusei Kishida, Ryuseikaku, 1952

■ *Tetsujin Garon* (*Writings of Tetsugoro Yorozu*), by Tetsugoro Yorozu, Chuo Koron Bijutsu Shuppan, 1968

■ *Nakagawa Kazumasa Bunshu* (*Writings of Nakagawa Kazumasa*)vol. 5. by Nakagawa Kazumasa, Chikuma Shobo, 1976

■ *Kishida Ryusei Zenshu* (*Complete writings of Ryusei Kishida*), vol. 7-8, by Ryusei Kishida, Iwanami Shoten, 1980

■ *Ryusei Nikki* (*Ryusei's diaries*), vol. 1-2, by Ryusei Kishida, Iwanami Shoten, 1984

Articles on Nojima Yasuzo

■ *Koga* vol. 1, no. 1-no. 6, Jurakusha, vol. 2, no. 1-12 Kogasha 1932-1933

■ *Ashiya Salon*, Ashiya camera club, 1935-1940

■ *Shashin tenrankai o mite* (*About the Photography exhibition*), by Kazuma Oda, Shashin Geppo, April, 1920

■ *Nojima shi no sakuhin ni tsuite* (*Mr. Nojima's works*), by Seison Yamazaki, Shashin geppo, April, 1920

■ *Kanso ; Nojima kun no sakuhin o mite* (*My Impressions of Mr, Nojima's works*), by Ryoka Kawakami, Shashin geppo, April, 1920

■ *Dai 10kai Shashin tenrankai dai 3 shitsu* (*The third room at the 10th photography exhibition*), by Mongaikan, Shashin Geppo, May, 1920

■ *Shashin tenrankai no hitotsu no keishiki toshite* (*One style of photography exhibition*), Hiromu Hara, Koga, August, 1933

■ *Nojima san no kingyou* (*Mr. Nojima's recent works*), by Kazumasa Nakagawa, Koga, August, 1933

■ *Shashin geppo, Nojima Yasuzo / Onna no kao* (*Monthly reviews, Yasuzo Nojima Women's Faces*), by Takaho Itagaki, Asahi Camera, August, 1965

■ *Zappo, Nojima Yasuzo Onna no Kao ten"(Notes, Yasuzo Nojima Women's Faces)*, Shashin geppo, August, 1965

■ *Gallery tenbyo, Nojima Yasuzo Kaikoten* (*Gallery reviews, Yasuzo Nojima retrospective exhibition*), Photoart, January, 1965

■ *Kongetsu no hiroba/Seikai data Nojima Yasuzo Kaikoten* (*Monthly reviews, Yasuzo Nojima retrospective exhibition received a good reputation*), Asahi Camera, January, 1965

■ *Nojima san no koto* (*Concerning Mr, Nojima*), by Toshio Fujii, Camera Mainichi, July, 1965

■ *Nudes- Yasuzo Nojima. Camera Mainichi*, July, 1965

■ *Ippin seisaku no omosa* (*The weight of one photograph*), by Seiji Otsuji, Camera Mainichi, January, 1969

■ *40nen mae no zennei shashin zashi Koga ga mezashita mono* (*What Koga was going to do 40 years ago*), Camera Mainichi, March, 1972

■ *Nojima Yasuzo san to Koga no shuhen* (*Mr. Yasuzo Nojima and his partners in Koga*), by Ihee Kimura, Camera Mainichi, March, 1972

■ *Nojima Yasuzo san to zashi Koga o shinobu kai* (*Memorial Party for Yasuzo Nojima and Koga*), Photoart, February, 1972

■ *Gendai shashin no genryu o tazunete 2 Nojima Yasuzo to Yasui Nakaji* (*Researching the origin of contemporary photography*), Asahi Camera, April Special isse, 1972

■ *Kimura Ihee Hodan shitsu 6. Showa hajime no shakaiha/tanbiha* (*Interview with Ihee Kimura vol. 6, Social photogra-*

phers and Art Photographers at the beginning of Showa), by Ihee Kimura, *Asahi Camera*, June, 1972

■ *Kimura Ihee Hodan shitsu 14. Shashin kaika ki no hito to sakuhin (Interview with Ihee Kimura vol. 14, Photographers and their works at the golden age of photography)*, by Ihee Kimura, *Asahi Camera*, February, 1973

■ *Hatan to houko-Nihon shashin 'Kindai' shiron 7. Yasuzo Nojima (Failure and losing the way-'Modernism' in Japanese photography)*, by Tatsuo Fukushima, *Fotoart*, September, 1974

■ *Shashin/Showa 50 nen shi 5, Nippon kindai shashin no yoake Koga to Nojima Yasuzo (History of Photography, 50 years of Showa* vol. 5, *the beginning of Modern photography in Japan, Koga* and Yasuzo Nojima), by Nobuo Ina, *Asahi Camera*, March, 1975

■ *Nojima Yasuzo to Koga (Nojima Yasuzo and Koga)*, by Kohtaro Iizawa, *ICONICS*, March, 1982

■ *Nihon kindai shashin no seiritsu 2 Nojima Yasuzo to Koga* (Establishment of Japanese modern photography, no. 2, *Yasuzo Nojima and Koga*), Toshiharu Ito, *Camera Mainichi*, April, 1983

■ *Shashin shi no shiza kara no. 7, Bunka no seijuku ni mukate-Stieglitz to Nojima Yasuzo (From the photo-hisitorical point of view-Stieghtz and Nojima)*, by Kohtaro Iizawa, *Asahi Camera*, July, 1985 *Koga ni tsuite (Concerning Koga)*, by Kohji Chige, *Annual Report of Hokkaido Kindai Bijutsukan*, March, 1986

■ *Antique image kan-Kindai shashin no kakuritsusha Nojima Yasuzo (Antique images, the founder of Japanese modern photography ; Yasuzo Nojima)*, by Kohtaro Iizawa, *Asahi Camera*, April, 1988

■ *Nojima Yasuzo no Geijutsu (The Art of Yasuzo Nojima)* by Jeffrey Gilbert, *Miru*, The National Museum of Modern Art, Kyoto, May, 1988

■ *Shashin de geijutsu! 1930 nendai Nippon no modern photo (Art by Photography, Japanese modern photography in 1930's)*, by Kohtaro Iizawa, *Geijutsu Shincho*, July, 1990

■ *Nakahara Teijiro to Nojima Yasuzo (Teijiro Nakahara and Yasuzo Nojima)*, by Toshiya Echizen, *Annual Report,* Hokkaido Asahikawa Bijitsukan Kiyo, March, 1989

■ *Shashinka ga eranda Showa no shashin best 10 (Best 10 photographers in Showa period selected by photographers)*, *Geijutsu Shincho*, July, 1989

■ *150 years of photographic art*, *Pacific Friend*, vol. 17, no. 8, 1989

■ *Sekai o tsukuta shozo shashin 100 mai (100 portraits making the international history)*, *Taiyo*, July, 1990

■ *Taisho ga unda 'Shashin bunka jin', Nojima Yasuzo (Photographer as an Intelligensia in Taisho period-Yasuzo Nojima)*, by Kohtaro Iizawa, *Geijitsu Shincho*, July, 1990

Exhibition Catalogs

■ *Nihon shashin 100 nen shi ten (The History of Japanese photography for 100 years)*, Nihon Shasinka Kyokai, 1962

■ *Shashin 100 nen-Nihonjin ni yoru shashin hyogen no rekishi (The History of art of Japanese photography for 100 years)* Nihon Shashinka Kyokai, 1975

■ *Gendai Nihon shashin shi ten (The History of Japanese Modern photography)*, Nihon Shashinka Kyokai, 1975

■ *Yasuzo Nojima*, Fermi National Accelerator Laboratory, Batavia, Illinois, 1979

■ *Geijutsu toshite no shashin-sono tanjo kara konnichi made (The Art of Photography, Past and Present, from the Collection of The Art Institute of Chicago)*, National Museum of Art, Osaka, 1984

■ *Tsukuba Shashin Bijutsukan '85 Paris, New York, Tokyo (Museum of Photography, Tsukuba '85 Paris, New York, Tokyo)*, Tsukuba Shashin Bijutsukan, 1985

■ *Japon des Avant-gardes 1910-1970*, Musée national d'art moderne, Centre George Pompidou, 1986

■ *Dai 60 Kai Kinen ten Kokugakai Shashinbu,(60th memorial exhibition, Kokugakai Photography Section)*, Kokugakai Shashinbu, 1986

■ *1920 nendai Nihon ten (The 1920's in Japan)*, Tokyo Metropolitan Museum of Art (tour), 1988-1989

■ *Nihon no shashin 1930 nendai ten (Japanese Photography in 1930's)*, The Museum of Modern Art, Kamakura, 1988

■ *Dai 63 kai 50 shunen kinen Kokugakai Shasinbu(The 63 rd memorial excibit, soth anniversary of the Kokugakai Photography section)*, Kokugakai Shashinbu, 1989

■ *Koga to sono jidai-1930 nendai no shozo shashin (Koga and its contemporary photographers-Portraits in 1930's)*, Asahi shimbunsha, 1989

■ *Shashin 150 nenten ·Torai kara konnichi made (150 years of Photography-from its influx to the Present)*, Shashin 150 nen ten Jikko Iinkai, 1989

■ *Seibutsu-Kotoba naki monotachi no saiten (The silent dialogue, Still life in the West and Japan)*, Shizuoka prefectual Museum of Art, 1990

■ *Shashin no Modernism (Modernism in Photography)*, Kokugakai Shashinbu, 1990

■ *La photographie japonaise de l'entre deux guerres, Du Pictorialisme au Modernisme*, Mission duPatrimoine Photographique, 1990

■ *On the Art of Fixing a Shadow : 150 years of Photography* National Gallery of Art, The Art Institute of Chicago, Los Angeles County Museum of Art, 1989.

■ *Shashin to Kaiga (Photography and Painting)* Tokyo Metropolitan Museum of Art, 1978

■ *Photographs from Chicago Collections*, The Art Institute of Chicago, 1982.

(Compiled by Yuri Mitsuda)

写真技法解説

野島康三の写真に見られるピグメント印画から近代的な銀塩印画への移行は、日本における写真技法の発展、普及の上からも興味深いものがある。

1930年以前の彼の作品の大部分はガム・プリント（ガム・バイクロメイト）によって制作されている。この技法は部分的な強調などの主観的な画像操作が可能であり、野島の初期の肖像写真《柳宗悦》などのように、被写体の個性を際だたせた印画が得られる。1930年頃から野島はブロムオイル・プリントの制作を始める。この技法は微妙な諸調を印画紙にもたらすことができる。1930年初頭に制作されたヌードの連作や《細川ちか子》などの肖像写真が持つ深い奥行きと厚みは、この技法の特性に負うところが大きい。特に《初秋》についてシカゴ美術館写真部長デヴィッド・トラビス氏は、「これ以上に優れたブロムオイル・プリントの例は無い」と絶賛している。

また野島は、一般的なゼラチンシルバー・プリント（銀塩プリント）も1930年代前半から制作を始めている。野島作品の転期を画した「女の顔」の連作はこの技法によって制作されている。

■ガム・プリント（ガム・バイクロメイト）

アラビアゴムに重クロム酸カリウムを混合した乳剤を感光剤として紙に塗布し、ネガを密着露光させる技法。乳剤は感光すると硬化して台紙に付着する。印画紙を水洗することで感光している部分は溶解し、台紙にポジの画像が残り定着される。この技法では乳剤に染料を混入させたり、台紙に乳剤の塗布・感光を繰り返すことで、一部分を強調した印画を制作することができる。

■ブロムオイル・プリント

ゼラチンと重クロム酸カリウムの感光硬化作用を利用する技法。印画紙には特殊なブロムオイル・ブロマイド紙が用いられる。この印画紙は露光・現像の後、漂白剤によって処理することで、表面にレリーフ状のネガ画像を得ることができる。この印画紙（版）に油性顔料を塗布し、紙を重ねて最終的な画像を転写する。ゼラチン部分の硬度（水分含有量）の差により、油性顔料の付着に差が生まれ、微妙で柔らかい諸調が得られる。版画のアクアチントと酷似したこの印画技法は、非常に高度な熟練を要する写真技法であるが、画面の諸調が自在に調整できることから、絵画主義写真を目指す世界中の写真家によって一時期多用された。

■ゼラチンシルバー・プリント

銀塩とゼラチン(塩化銀／臭化銀ゼラチン印画紙)を感光乳剤として用いる印画法で、今日広く普及している一般的な白黒写真印画の技法。1920年代以後の近代写真の確立期には、そのストレートな材質感が写真の特性を端的に表現し、絵画とは独立した写真の独自性を確立する上で重要な役割を果たした。

作品リスト

凡例：
野島康三写真作品は目録番号21を除きすべて、野島康三遺作保存会所蔵・京都国立近代美術館寄託のものである。目録番号 1 —104の作品データは、目録番号／作品名／制作年／寸法(mm,高さ×幅)／技法／署名・年記／野島コレクション・コード番号、または所蔵者の順である。
目録番号105—144の油彩および素描の作品は、作品名／制作年／寸法(mm,高さ×幅)／技法／作品出品歴／所蔵者の順である。なお作品出品歴は、特に野島康三と交流の深かった時期のもののみを記載した。

1
にごれる海
1910
173×242
ガム・プリント
台紙裏に題名、撮影年記、制作年記
NY-A14

2
大磯にて
1912
146×191
オゾブロム・プリント
画面に署名、年記／裏面に題名、署名、年記
NY-A66

3
銚子にて
1915
112×148
ガム・プリント
画面に署名、年記／裏面に題名、年記
NY-A49

4
髪梳く女
1914
285×231
ガム・プリント
画面に署名、年記
NY-A1

5
樹による女
1915
289×217
ガム・プリント
画面に署名、年記
NY-A2

6
題名不詳
1920
274×232
ガム・プリント
裏面に日付け
NY-A3

7
立てる女
1917
280×207
ガム・プリント
画面に年記／裏面に署名、年記
NY-A4

8
女
1918
248×168
ガム・プリント
画面に署名、年記／裏面に年記
NY-A5

9
題名不詳
1920
150×98
ガム・プリント

裏面に年記
NY-A50

10
題名不詳
1921
285×214
ガム・プリント
参紙裏に年記、署名
NY-A90

11
裸婦
1921
155×144
ガム・プリント
裏面に署名、年記
NY-A91

12
題名不詳
1921
244×172
ガム・プリント
裏面に署名、年記
NY-A6

13
風邪の少年
1920
283×239
ガム・プリント
裏面に題名、署名、年記
NY-A11

14
題名不詳
1915
224×227
ガム・プリント
NY-A81

15
題名不詳
1921
273×230
ガム・プリント
裏面に年記
NY-A7

16
S氏肖像
1921
269×184
ガム・プリント
NY-A51

17
錦古里孝治氏
1920
279×215
ガム・プリント
裏面に年記
NY-A52

18
M氏肖像
1917
288×244
ガム・プリント

画面に署名、年記
NY-A40・2

19
中川一政氏
1923
212×165
ガム・プリント
裏面に年記
NY-A12

20
柳宋悦氏
1923
292×238
ガム・プリント
台紙裏に題名、年記
NY-A13

21
富本憲吉氏
1925
283×235
ガム・プリント
日本大学芸術学部写真学科蔵

22
題名不詳
1930
280×216
ブロムオイル・プリント
台紙裏に年記
NY-A82

23
題名不詳
1930
256×231
ブロムオイル・プリント
裏面に年記
NY-A70

24
題名不詳
1930
280×235
ブロムオイル・プリント
裏面に年記
NY-A93

25
題名不詳
1930
272×202
ブロムオイル・プリント
台紙裏に年記
NY-A67

26
漁夫肖像
1930
368×269
ブロムオイル・プリント
裏面に年記、題名
NY-A144

27
慈姑の図
1927
210×283

画面に署名、年記
ブロムオイル・プリント
裏面に署名、年記、題名
NY-A16

28
仏手柑
1930
172×275
ブロムオイル・プリント
裏面に題名、年記
NY-A134

29
題名不詳
1930
256×377
ブロムオイル・プリント
裏面に年記
NY-A136

30
題名不詳
1930
226×242
ブロムオイル・プリント
裏面に年記
NY-A135

31
題名不詳
1930
265×406
ブロムオイル・プリント
台紙裏に年記
NY-A39

32
枇杷
1930
233×398
ブロムオイル・プリント
裏面に年記、題名
NY-A137

33
和子
1931
388×295
ブロムオイル・プリント
裏面に年記、題名
NY-A64

34
庭にて
1930
300×405
ブロムオイル・プリント
台紙裏に署名、題名、年記
NY-A89

35
初秋
1930
274×392
ブロムオイル・プリント
裏面に年記
NY-A141

36
樹

1930
283×217
ブロムオイル・プリント
裏面に署名、年記、題名
NY-A54

37
樹
1930
298×235
ブロムオイル・プリント
裏面に署名、年記、題名
NY-A55

38
題名不詳
1930
374×276
ブロムオイル・プリント
台紙裏に署名、年記、題名
NY-A59

39
題名不詳
1926
213×289
ブロムオイル・プリント
台紙裏に年記
NY-A53

40
題名不詳
1930
248×299
ブロムオイル・プリント
裏面に年記
NY-A9

41
仕事場
1930
310×414
ブロムオイル・プリント
裏面に署名、年記、題名
NY-A142

42
仕事場、土こね
1930
271×401
ブロムオイル・プリント
台紙裏に題名、年記、署名
NY-A131

43
仕事場、鋳物
1930
381×229
ブロムオイル・プリント
裏面に署名、年記、題名
NY-A130

44
裸の背中
1930
398×276
ブロムオイル・プリント
裏面に題名、年記
NY-A24

45
裸胸婦
1930
408×274
ブロムオイル・プリント
裏面に年記、題名
NY-A23

46
裸婦
1930
253×334
ブロムオイル・プリント
台紙裏に署名、年記、題名
NY-A26

47
題名不詳
1931
386×268
ブロムオイル・プリント
裏面に年記
NY-A29

48
題名不詳
1931
275×405
ブロムオイル・プリント
裏面に年記
NY-A30

49
題名不詳
1931
395×269
ブロムオイル・プリント
裏面に年記
NY-A27

50
題名不詳
1931
293×322
ブロムオイル・プリント
裏面に年記
NY-A31

51
題名不詳
1931
303×418
ブロムオイル・プリント
NY-A124

52
題名不詳
1931
315×415
ブロムオイル・プリント
台紙裏に年記
NY-A129

53
題名不詳
1932
324×413
ブロムオイル・プリント
裏面に年記
NY-A28

54
題名不詳
1931
414×309
ブロムオイル・プリント
台紙裏に年記
NY-A33

55
題名不詳
1931
414×336
ブロムオイル・プリント
台紙裏に年記
NY-A35

56
題名不詳
1931
309×409
ブロムオイル・プリント
裏面に年記
NY-A25

57
T嬢
1931
412×272
ブロムオイル・プリント
裏面に年記
NY-A41

58
題名不詳
1931
412×270
ブロムオイル・プリント
裏面に年記
NY-A42

59
題名不詳
1932
410×338
ブロムオイル・プリント
裏面に年記
NY-A37

60
肖像(モデルF)
1931
384×307
ブロムオイル・プリント
台紙裏に題名、署名、年記
NY-A108

61
題名不詳(モデルF)
1931
389×338
ブロムオイル・プリント
裏面に年記
NY-A78

62
肖像(モデルF)
1931
333×271
ブロムオイル・プリント
台紙裏に署名、題名、年記

NY-A80

63
題名不詳(モデルF)
1931
396×306
ブロムオイル・プリント
裏面に年記
NY-A109

64
題名不詳(モデルF)
1931
325×295
ブロムオイル・プリント
台紙裏に年記
NY-A101

65
題名不詳(モデルF)
1931
412×333
ブロムオイル・プリント
台紙裏に年記
NY-A103

66
題名不詳(モデルF)
1931
401×328
ブロムオイル・プリント
裏面に年記
NY-A104

67
題名不詳(モデルF)
1931
374×311
ブロムオイル・プリント
裏面に年記
NY-A77

68
顔(モデルF)
1931
385×278
ブロムオイル・プリント
台紙に署名、題名、年記
NY-A79

69
題名不詳(モデルF)
1931
410×338
ブロムオイル・プリント
裏面に年記
NY-A36

70
女(モデルF)
1931
409×333
ブロムオイル・プリント
台紙裏に署名、年記
NY-A125

71
顔
1931
376×326

ブロムオイル・プリント
台紙裏に署名、年記、題名
NY-A74

72
坐婦人像
1931
390×270
ブロムオイル・プリント
台紙裏に署名、年記、題名
NY-A75

73
モデルE
1931
414×336
ブロムオイル・プリント
裏面に題名、年記
NY-A123

74
細川ちか子氏
1932
407×307
ブロムオイル・プリント
裏面に年記、題名
NY-A19

75
細川ちか子氏
1932
411×276
ブロムオイル・プリント
裏面に年記、題名
NY-A94

76
千田是也氏
1932
404×316
ブロムオイル・プリント
裏面に年記、題名
NY-A133

77
バイオリニスト・ポーラック氏
1931
412×330
ブロムオイル・プリント
裏面に年記、題名
NY-A85

78
千田夫人
1932
407×332
ブロムオイル・プリント
裏面に年記、題名
NY-A132

79
題名不詳
1931
374×256
ブロムオイル・プリント
台紙裏に年記
NY-A72

80
題名不詳

1932
412×326
ブロムオイル・プリント
裏面に年記
NY-A73

81
題名不詳
1931-32
558×458
ゼラチンシルバー・プリント
NY-A114

82
題名不詳
1931-32
557×461
ゼラチンシルバー・プリント
NY-A111

83
題名不詳
1931-32
540×416
ゼラチンシルバー・プリント
NY-A115

84
題名不詳
1931-32
555×440
ゼラチンシルバー・プリント
NY-A116

85
題名不詳
1931-32
544×402
ゼラチンシルバー・プリント
NY-A121

86
T嬢
1933
555×453
ゼラチンシルバー・プリント
裏面に年記
NY-A128

87
女
1932
556×431
ゼラチンシルバー・プリント
裏面に年記
NY-A110

88
題名不詳
1931-32
558×458
ゼラチンシルバー・プリント
NY-A113

89
題名不詳
1931-32
558×440
ゼラチンシルバー・プリント
NY-A127

90
女
1933
557×450
ゼラチンシルバー・プリント
裏面に年記
NY-A118

91
女
c. 1931
554×425
ゼラチンシルバー・プリント
NY-B80

92
題名不詳
1938-40
550×415
ゼラチンシルバー・プリント
NY-A44

93
女
1933
358×348
ゼラチンシルバー・プリント
裏面に署名、年記
NY-B23

94
女
1933
379×354
ゼラチンシルバー・プリント
裏面に年記
NY-A126

95
静物
c. 1935
255×267
ゼラチンシルバー・プリント
裏面に題名、署名
NY-B3

96
題名不詳(モデルF)
1933
543×427
ゼラチンシルバー・プリント
裏面に年記
NY-B91

97
題名不詳
1933
538×448
ゼラチンシルバー・プリント
裏面に年記
NY-B67

98
女
1933
545×443
ゼラチンシルバー・プリント
裏面に年記
NY-B64

99
チューリップ
1940
542×449
ゼラチンシルバー・プリント
裏面に出品歴
NY-A46

100
ぎんれい花
1941
551×452
ゼラチンシルバー・プリント
裏面に年記
NY-A146

101
ぎんれい花
1939
468×403
ゼラチンシルバー・プリント
裏面に題名、年記
NY-B75

102
ぎんれい花
1941
543×453
ゼラチンシルバー・プリント
裏面に年記
NY-A47

103
薄、軽井沢にて
c. 1940
412×518
ゼラチンシルバー・プリント
裏面に署名、題名
NY-A48

104
てぶくろ
1951
435×464
ゼラチンシルバー・プリント
裏面に署名、題名、年記
NY-B76

作品リスト No.104-144 は
p.173 へ続く

NOTES:
All photographic works except catalog No. 21 by Yasuzo Nojima are courtesy of The National Museum of Modern Art, Kyoto from extended loan by The Nojima Collection.
The data for the works No. 1-104 are arranged in the following order: catalogue No. /title/date/size (mm, h×w)/medium/marks/Nojima Collection # or lender.   The data for the works No. 105-144 are arranged: Title/date/size (mm, h×w)/medium/lenders

1
Muddy Sea
1910
173×242
Gum Bichromate Print
title, date on mount verso
NY-A14

2
At Ooiso
1912
146×191
Ozobrome Print
signed, date on print surface/title,
signed, date on print verso
NY-A66

3
At Choshi
1915
112×148
Gum Bichromate Print
signed, date on print surface/title,
date on print verso
NY-A49

4
Woman Combing Her Hair
1914
285×231
Gum Bichromate Print
signed, date on print surface
NY-A1

5
Woman Leaning on a Tree
1915
289×217
Gum Bichromate Print
signed, date on print surface
NY-A2

6
Title Unknown
1920
274×232
Gum Bichromate Print
date on print verso
NY-A3

7
Standing Woman
1917
280×207
Gum Bichromate Print
date on print surface/signed, date
on print verso
NY-A4

8
Woman
1918
248×168
Gum Bichromate Print
signed, date on print surface/date
on print verso
NY-A5

9
Title Unknown
1920
150×98
Gum Bichromate Print
date on print verso
NY-A50

10
Title Unknown
1921
285×214
Gum Bichromate Print
signed, date on mount verso
NY-A90

11
Nude
1921
155×144
Gum Bichromate Print
signed, date on print verso
NY-A91

12
Title Unknown
1921
244×172
Gum Bichromate Print
signed, date on print verso
NY-A6

13
Boy with a Cold
1920
283×239
Gum Bichromate Print
title, date, signed on print verso
NY-A11

14
Title Unknown
1915
224×227
Gum Bichromate Print
NY-A81

15
Title Unknown
1921
273×230
Gum Bichromate Print
date on print verso
NY-A7

16
Portrait of Mr. S.
1921
269×184
Gum Bichromate Print
NY-A51

17
Mr. Koji Nishigori
1920
279×215
Gum Bichromate Print
date on print verso
NY-A52

18
Portrait of Mr. M.
1917
288×244
Gum Bichromate Print
signed, date on print surface
NY-A40·2

19
Mr. Kazumasa Nakagawa
1923
212×165
Gum Bichromate Print
date on print verso

NY-A12

20
Mr. Muneyoshi (Soetsu) Yanagi
1923
292×238
Gum Bichromate Print
title, date on mount verso
NY-A13

21
Mr. Kenkichi Tomimoto
1925
283×235
Gum Bichromate Print
Nihon University, Department of
Photography, College of Art

22
Title Unknown
1930
280×216
Bromoil Print
date on mount verso
NY-A82

23
Title Unknown
1930
256×231
Bromoil Print
date on print verso
NY-A70

24
Title Unknown
1930
280×235
Bromoil Print
date on print verso
NY-A93

25
Title Unknown
1930
272×202
Bromoil Print
date on mount verso
NY-A67

26
Portrait of a Fisherman
1930
368×269
Bromoil Print
title, date on print verso
NY-A144

27
Water Chestnuts
1927
210×283
Bromoil Print
signed, date, title on print verso
NY-A16

28
Bushukan
1930
172×275
Bromoil Print
title, date on print verso
NY-A134

29
Title Unknown

1930
256×377
Bromoil Print
date on print verso
NY-A136

30
Title Unknown
1930
226×242
Bromoil Print
date on print verso
NY-A135

31
Title Unknown
1930
265×406
Bromoil Print
date on mount verso
NY-A39

32
Loquats
1930
233×398
Bromoil Print
date, title on print verso
NY-A137

33
Kazuko
1931
388×295
Bromoil Print
date, title on print verso
NY-A64

34
In the Garden
1930
300×405
Bromoil Print
signed, title, date on mount verso
NY-A89

35
Early Autumn
1930
274×392
Bromoil Print
date on print verso
NY-A141

36
Tree
1930
283×217
Bromoil Print
signed, title, date on print verso
NY-A54

37
Tree
1930
298×235
Bromoil Print
signed, title, date on mount verso
NY-A55

38
Title Unknown
1930
374×276
Bromoil Print
signed, title, date on mount verso

NY-A59

39
Title Unknown
1926
213×289
Bromoil Print
date on mount verso
NY-A53

40
Title Unknown
1930
248×299
Bromoil Print
date on print verso
NY-A9

41
Workshop
1930
310×414
Bromoil Print
signed, date, title on print verso
NY-A142

42
Workshop, Wedging Clay
1930
271×401
Bromoil Print
title, date, signed on mount verso
NY-A131

43
Casting Workshop
1930
381×229
Bromoil Print
signed, title, date on print verso
NY-A130

44
Nude from Rear
1930
398×276
Bromoil Print
title, date on print verso
NY-A24

45
Nude Torso
1930
408×274
Bromoil Print
date, signed on print verso
NY-A23

46
Nude
1930
253×334
Bromoil Print
signed, title, date on mount verso
NY-A26

47
Title Unknown
1931
386×268
Bromoil Print
date on print verso
NY-A29

48
Title Unknown

1931
275×405
Bromoil Print
date on print verso
NY-A30

49
Title Unknown
1931
395×269
Bromoil Print
date on print verso
NY-A27

50
Title Unknown
1931
293×322
Bromoil Print
date on print verso
NY-A31

51
Title Unknown
1931
303×418
Bromoil Print
NY-A124

52
Title Unknown
1931
315×415
Bromoil Print
date on mount verso
NY-A129

53
Title Unknown
1932
324×413
Bromoil Print
date on print verso
NY-A28

54
Title Unknown
1931
414×309
Bromoil Print
date on mount verso
NY-A33

55
Title Unknown
1931
414×336
Bromoil Print
date on mount verso
NY-A35

56
Title Unknown
1931
309×409
Bromoil Print
date on print verso
NY-A25

57
Miss T.
1931
412×272
Bromoil Print
date on print verso
NY-A41

58
Title Unknown
1931
412×270
Bromoil Print
date on print verso
NY-A42

59
Title Unknown
1932
410×338
Bromoil Print
date on print verso
NY-A37

60
Portrait (Model F.)
1931
384×307
Bromoil Print
title, signed, date on mount verso
NY-A108

61
Title Unknown (Model F.)
1931
389×338
Bromoil Print
date on print verso
NY-A78

62
Portrait (Model F.)
1931
333×271
Bromoil Print
signed, title, date on mount verso
NY-A80

63
Title Unknown (Model F.)
1931
396×306
Bromoil Print
date on print verso
NY-A109

64
Title Unknown (Model F.)
1931
325×295
Bromoil Print
date on mount verso
NY-A101

65
Title Unknown (Model F.)
1931
412×333
Bromoil Print
date on mount verso
NY-A103

66
Title Unknown (Model F.)
1931
401×328
Bromoil Print
date on print verso
NY-A104

67
Title Unknown (Model F.)
1931
374×311

Bromoil Print
date on print verso
NY-A77

68
Face (Model F.)
1931
385×278
Bromoil Print
signed, title, date on mount verso
NY-A79

69
Title Unknown (Model F.)
1931
410×338
Bromoil Print
date on print verso
NY-A36

70
Woman (Model F.)
1931
409×333
Bromoil Print
signed, date on mount verso
NY-A125

71
Face
1931
376×326
Bromoil Print
signed, date, title on mount verso
NY-A74

72
Seated Female Figure
1931
390×270
Bromoil Print
signed, title, date on mount verso
NY-A75

73
Model E.
1931
414×336
Bromoil Print
title, date on print verso
NY-A123

74
Miss Chikako Hosokawa
1932
407×307
Bromoil Print
date, title on print verso
NY-A19

75
Miss Chikako Hosokawa
1932
411×276
Bromoil Print
date, title on print verso
NY-A94

76
Mr. Koreya Senda
1932
404×316
Bromoil Print
date, title on print verso
NY-A133

77
Mr. Pollack, Violinist
1931
412×330
Bromoil Print
date, title on print verso
NY-A85

78
Mrs. Koreya Senda
1932
407×332
Bromoil Print
date, title on print verso
NY-A132

79
Title Unknown
1931
374×256
Bromoil Print
date on mount verso
NY-A72

80
Title Unknown
1932
412×326
Bromoil Print
date on print verso
NY-A73

81
Title Unknown
1931-32
558×458
Gelatin Silver Print
NY-A114

82
Title Unknown
1931-32
557×461
Gelatin Silver Print
NY-A111

83
Title Unknown
1931-32
540×416
Gelatin Silver Print
NY-A115

84
Title Unknown
1931-32
555×440
Gelatin Silver Print
NY-A116

85
Title Unknown
1931-32
544×402
Gelatin Silver Print
NY-A121

86
Miss T.
1933
555×453
Gelatin Silver Print
title, date on print verso
NY-A128

87

Woman
1932
556×431
Gelatin Silver Print
date on print verso
NY-A110

88
Title Unknown
1931-32
558×458
Gelatin Silver Print
NY-A113

89
Title Unknown
1931-32
558×440
Gelatin Silver Print
NY-A127

90
Woman
1933
557×450
Gelatin Silver Print
date on print verso
NY-A118

91
Woman
c. 1931
554×425
Gelatin Silver Print
NY-B80

92
Title Unknown
1938-40
550×415
Gelatin Silver Print
NY-A44

93
Woman
1933
358×348
Gelatin Silver Print
signed, date, print verso
NY-B23

94
Woman
1933
379×354
Gelatin Silver Print
date on print verso
NY-A126

95
Still Life
c. 1935
255×267
Gelatin Silver Print
title, signed, marks on print verso
NY-B3

96
Title Unknown (Model F.)
1933
543×427
Gelatin Silver Print
date on print verso
NY-B91

97

Title Unknown
1933
538×448
Gelatin Silver Print
date on print verso
NY-B67

98
Woman
1933
545×443
Gelatin Silver Print
date on print verso
NY-B64

99
Tulip
1940
542×449
Gelatin Silver Print
marks on print verso
NY-A46

100
Ginreika
1941
551×452
Gelatin Silver Print
date on print verso
NY-A146

101
Ginreika
1939
468×403
Gelatin Silver Print
title, date on print verso
NY-B75

102
Ginreika
1941
543×453
Gelatin Silver Print
date on print verso
NY-A47

103
Susuki Grass at Karuizawa
c. 1940
412×518
Gelatin Silver Print
signed, title on print verso
NY-A48

104
Gloves
1951
435×464
Gelatin Silver Print
signed, title, date on print verso
NY-B76

Check list no.105-144
continue on page 174

野島康三と同時代の画家たち

野島康三

105
題名不詳(風景)
1926
315×395
油彩、麻布
個人蔵

106
びわ
1926
244×410
油彩、麻布
個人蔵

107
題名不詳(裸婦Ⅰ)
n. d.
250×177
油彩、麻布
個人蔵

108
題名不詳(裸婦Ⅱ)
n. d.
250×177
油彩、麻布
個人蔵

岸田劉生

109
裸婦(トルソー)
1913
440×590
油彩、麻布
第1回生活社主催油絵展(1913)
大原美術館蔵

110
川幡正光氏之肖像
1918
335×335
油彩、麻布
第6回草土社展(1918)
東京国立近代美術館蔵

111
南瓜を持てる女
1914
800×575
油彩、麻布
岸田劉生作品展覧会
(1914、田中屋)
ブリヂストン美術館蔵

112
画家の妻
1914
580×538
油彩、麻布
個人蔵

113
村娘之図
1919
450×334

水彩、木炭、紙
第7回草土社展(1919)
下関市立美術館蔵

114
童児肖像
1921
340×255
水彩、紙
さえぐさ画廊蔵／東京国立近代美術館
寄託

115
野童女
1922
640×520
油彩、麻布
岸田劉生個人展覧会(1922、野島邸)
個人蔵／神奈川県立近代美術館寄託

116
壺
1916
378×267
油彩、板
第3回草土社展(1916)
下関市立美術館蔵

117
初夏の小路
1917
445×365
油彩、麻布
第4回二科会展(1917)
下関市立美術館蔵

118
林檎三個
1917
318×410
油彩、麻布
第4回草土社展(1917)
個人蔵

119
静物
1920
365×440
油彩、麻布
大原美術館蔵

梅原龍三郎

120
坐裸婦
1918
325×500
油彩、麻布
第7回二科会展(1920)
東京国立近代美術館蔵

121
裸婦
1936
806×660
油彩、麻布
第12回大阪国画会展(1938)
ひろしま美術館蔵

122
竹窓裸婦

1937
890×710
油彩、麻布
梅原龍三郎新作油絵展(1938、高島
屋)
大原美術館蔵

123
豹裸婦
1926
290×444
油彩、麻布
国画創作協会展(1927)
下関市立美術館蔵

124
裸婦図
1929
410×493
油彩、麻布
メナード美術館蔵

125
熱海野島別荘
1933
626×778
油彩、麻布
神奈川県立近代美術館蔵

126
熱海風景
1935
735×610
油彩、麻布
メナード美術館蔵

萬鐵五郎

127
雲のある自画像
1912
595×490
油彩、麻布
大原美術館蔵

128
自画像
1915
495×333
油彩、麻布
宮城県美術館蔵

129
習作
1913
452×328
油彩、麻布
大原美術館蔵

130
雲と裸婦
1922
240×160
油彩、麻布
ギャラリー新居蔵

131
裸婦
1918
450×330
油彩、麻布

神奈川県立近代美術館蔵

132
ほほ杖の人
1926
1170×800
油彩、麻布
第4回春陽会展(1925)
東京国立近代美術館蔵

133
雪の景
1915
610×730
油彩、麻布
第2回日本美術家協会展(1917)
新潟県立美術博物館蔵

134
雪景色
c.1915
455×335
油彩、麻布
財団法人中野美術館蔵

135
丘の道
1918
390×445
油彩、麻布
萬鐵五郎記念館蔵

136
湘南風景
1926
490×593
油彩、麻布
第4回春陽会展(1926)
東京国立近代美術館蔵

中川一政

137
春光
1915
377×455
油彩、麻布
中川一政個人展覧会(1920、兜屋畫
堂)
真鶴町立中川一政美術館蔵

138
杉と茶畑
1916
457×530
油彩、麻布
中川一政個人展覧会(1920、兜屋畫
堂)
真鶴町立中川一政美術館蔵

139
夕日が落ちる小さい踏切
1917
458×522
油彩、麻布
第5回草土社展(1917)
個人蔵

140
監獄裏の落目
1919

456×530
油彩、麻布
第6回二科会展会(1919)
群馬県立近代美術館蔵

141
夏
1918
450×530
油彩、麻布
第5回二科会展(1918)
財団法人清春白樺美術館蔵

142
冬日路傍
1924
497×604
油彩、麻布
財団法人清春白樺美術館蔵

143
初夏水辺
1919
456×531
油彩、麻布
中川一政個人展覧会(1920、兜屋畫堂)
個人蔵

144
柚子壜図
1925
225×320
油彩、麻布
雅陶堂ギャラリー蔵

出品資料リスト

［出版物］
1：野島康三遺作集／日本写真センター発行／昭和40年(1965)／52作品収録／野島康三遺作保存会蔵
2：写真月報第25巻第4号／写真月報社発行／大正9年4月(1920)／「朱雪雑記・野島煕正」他を収録／金子隆一氏蔵
3：中原梯二郎作品集／日本美術院発行／大正10年(1921)／野島康三撮影写真62葉収録／渋谷区立松濤美術館蔵
4：富木憲吉模様集（3分冊）／自家出版／昭和2年(1927)／野島康三撮影写真192葉収録／伊砂利彦氏蔵
5：アルス写真大講座第二巻／アルス社刊／昭和4年(1929)／「人物作画法・野島煕正」収録／金子隆一氏蔵
6：光画／聚楽社・光画社発行／昭和7年5月―昭和8年12月（全18号）／飯沢耕太郎氏蔵
7：関根正二遺作展画集／兜屋畫堂発行／大正8年(1919)／時の美術社蔵
8：梅原龍三郎画集／春鳥会発行／昭和12年(1937)／「アトリエの一日」野島康三撮影写真10葉収録／東京都美術館蔵

［印刷物］
9：岸田劉生個人展覧会出品目録／大正11年(1922)／野島康三遺作保存

会蔵
10：萬鐵五郎日本画展覧会案内状／大正11年／野島康三遺作保存会蔵
11：ノノミヤ・アパートメント・パンフレット／野島康三遺作保存会蔵

NOJIMA AND CONTEMPORARIES

Yasuzo Nojima

105
Title Unknown (Landscape)
1926
315×395
oil on canvas
Private Collection

106
Loquats
1926
244×410
oil on canvas
Private Collection

107
Title Unknown (Nude I)
n. d.
250×177
oil on canvas
Private Collection

108
Title Unknown (Nude II)
n. d.
250×177
oil on canvas
Private Collection

Ryusei Kishida

109
Nude (Torso)
1913
440×590
oil on canvas
Ohara Museum of Art

110
Portrait of Masamitsu Kawabata
1918
335×335
oil on canvas
The National Museum of Modern Art, Tokyo

111
Woman with a Squash
1914
800×575
oil on canvas
Bridgestone Museum of Art

112
Portrait of the Artist's Wife
1914
580×538
oil on canvas
Private Collection

113
Portrait of a Village Girl
1919
450×334
watercolor, charcoal on paper
Shimonoseki City Museum

114
Portrait of a Little Boy
1921
340×255
watercolor on paper

Saegusa Gallery／Deposit at The
National Museum of Modern Art,
Tokyo

115
Possessed Little Girl
1922
640×520
oil on canvas
Deposit at The Museum of Modern
Art, Kamakura

116
Urn
1916
378×267
oil on boad
Shimonoseki City Museum

117
Lane in Early Summer
1917
445×365
oil on canvas
Simonoseki City Museum

118
Three Apples
1917
318×410
oil on canvas
Private Collection

119
Still Life
1920
365×440
oil on canvas
Ohara Museum of Art

Ryuzaburo Umehara

120
Seated Nude
1918
325×500
oil on canvas
The National Museum of Art,
Tokyo

121
Nude
1936
806×660
oil on canvas
Hiroshima Museum of Art

122
Nude by the Window
1937
890×710
oil on canvas
Ohara Museum of Art

123
Nude with a Leopard Skin
1926
290×444
oil on canvas
Shimonoseki City Museum

124
Nude
1929
410×493
oil on canvas

Menard Art Museum

125
Nojima Villa at Atami
1933
626×778
oil on canvas
The Museum of Modern Art,
Kamakura

126
Atami
1935
735×610
oil on canvas
Menard Art Museum

Tetsugoro Yorozu

127
Self-portrait with Clouds
1912
595×490
oil on canvas
Ohara Museum of Art

128
Self-portrait
1915
495×333
oil on canvas
Miyagi Museum of Art

129
Study
1913
452×328
oil on canvas
Ohara Museum of Art

130
Clouds and Nude
1922
240×160
oil on canvas
Courtesy of Gallery Nii, Osaka

131
Nude
1918
450×330
oil on canvas
The Museum of Modern Art,
Kamakura

132
Nude (Resting Her Chin on Hand)
1926
1170×800
oil on canvas
The National Museum of Modern
Art, Tokyo

133
Snow Landscape
1915
610×730
oil on canvas
Nigata Prefectural Museum of Art

134
Snow Landscape
c.1915
455×335
oil on canvas
Nakano Art Museum

135
Road in the Hill
1918
390×445
oil on canvas
Yorozu Tetsugoro Museum

136
Landscape of Shonan
1926
490×593
oil on canvas
The National Museum of Modern
Art, Tokyo

Kazumasa Nakagawa

137
Spring Light
1915
377×455
oil on canvas
Kazumasa Nakagawa Art
Museum, Manazuru

138
Cedar and Tea-field
1916
457×530
oil on canvas
Kazumasa Nakagawa Art
Museum, Manazuru

139
Setting Sun at a Small Crossing
1917
458×522
oil on canvas
Private Collection

140
Setting Sun from Back of a Prison
1919
456×530
oil on canvas
Gunma Prefectural Museum of
Modern Art

141
L'été
1918
450×530
oil on canvas
Kiyoharu Shirakaba Museum

142
L'hiver—au bord de la route
1924
497×604
oil on canvas
Kiyoharu Shirakaba Museum

143
Waterside in Early Summer
1919
456×531
oil on canvas
Private Collection

144
Picture of Citrons and a Bottle
1925
225×320
oil on canvas
Courtesy of Gatodo Gallery, Tokyo

Photographs were supplied by the lenders, however, the following
photographers and providers are acknowledged (numbers refer
to catalogue entries).
Harumi Konishi (小西晴美)／No. 1-20, No. 22-104
BSS (美術出版デザインセンター)／No. 119, 122, 127, 129
Sakamoto Photo Research Lab. (坂本万七写真研究所)／No. 114
Okamura Printing Industry (岡村印刷工業株式会社)／No. 137, 138
Yoshii Gallery (吉井画廊)／No. 143
Nichido Gallery (日動面廊)／No. 118

野島康三とその周辺

編集——————河本信治／京都国立近代美術館
　　　　　　　　光田由里／渋谷区立松濤美術館
発行——————京都国立近代美術館
　　　　　　　　渋谷区立松濤美術館
ブック・デザイン— 西岡　勉
印刷——————日本写真印刷株式会社
著作権者————京都国立近代美術館
　　　　　　　　渋谷区立松濤美術館
　　　　　　　　©1991

YASUZO NOJIMA AND CONTEMPORARIES

edited by————Shinji Kohmoto, The National Museum of Modern Art, Kyoto
　　　　　　　　Yuri Mitsuda, The Shoto Museum of Art
Published by——The National Muneum of Art, Kyoto
　　　　　　　　The Shoto Museum of Art
book design———Tsutomu Nishioka
printed by————Nissha Printing Co., Ltd
copyright————The National Museum of Modern Art, Kyoto
　　　　　　　　The Shoto Museum of Art
　　　　　　　　© 1991

ISBN 4-87642-129-3